FEMINIST PEDAGOGY
AN AUTOBIOGRAPHICAL APPROACH

ANNE-LOUISE BROOKES

FERNWOOD PUBLISHING

HALIFAX

Copyright © 1992 by Anne-Louise Brookes

All right reserved. No part of this book may be reproduced or transmitted in any form by any means without permission in writing from the publisher, except by a reviewer, who may quote brief passages in a review.

Editing: Jane Butler
Cover illustration: Joanne Sinclair
Design and production: Beverley Rach
Printed and bound in Canada.

A publication of:
Fernwood Publishing
Box 9409, Station A
Halifax, Nova Scotia
B3K 5S3

Canadian Cataloguing in Publication Data

Brookes, Anne-Louise, 1944-

    Feminist pedagogy

    Based on the author's thesis (Ph.D.--University of Toronto)
    Includes bibliographical references.
    ISBN 1-895686-00-8

1. Teaching -- Psychological aspects.
2. Education -- Social aspects. I. Title.

LB1027.B76 1992   370'.1   C92-098575-0

for Elsie Augusta

contents

Acknowledgements

Preamble / 1

   A. Fragments / 1

Introduction / 7

   A. Subjects In/Formation: Problems and Perspectives / 7

Chapter one / 15

   A. Breaking the Silence / 15
   B. Breaking the Sequence / 17
   C. Re-Visioning the Past / 27

Chapter two / 33

   A. Crises and Contradictions: Re-viewing Ideology / 33
   B. Re-Confronting the Limits of Social Knowledge:
     (my own, in particular) / 38
   C. Breaking the Cycle/Circle / 40

Chapter three / 43

   A. Perspectives and Approaches / 43
   B. Feminist Pedagogy In/Formation / 47
   C. Punctuating the Dominant Order / 55

Chapter four / 63

A. Re-Visioning through the Gaps and Cracks / 63
B. Theorizing Memories / 66
C. In/Forming Issues and Subjects / 68
D. Problematizing Experience:
   One Viewer Re-Viewing the Past / 70
E. Re-Visioning Anew / 75

Chapter five / 81

A. Glimmerings into the Dark / 81
B. Peace and War: Absenting the Subject / 89
C. Glimmerings into the Light / 97

Chapter six / 101

A. Contradictions and a Desire for Harmony / 101
B. Re-Considering the Binding and Unbinding
   of Ideological Practices / 107
C. (Some) Re-Considerations / 123

Chapter seven / 129

A. Reading From the Margins / 129
B. Writing from the Margins / 133
C. An(other) Feminist Analysis of the Fallout / 140

Chapter eight / 147

A. Some End(ings) / 147
B. Another End(ing) / 153
C. Beginning Again: Doing Class / 154
D. Endings of Another Kind / 160

References / 161

acknowledgements

Many centuries of women's struggle precede and, indeed, make possible this work. The love of a few enabled me to write. From my heart, I thank you.

I owe a special thanks to many people for the completion of this book. The cover illustration is the work of Joanne Sinclair who also typed the manuscript. I am grateful to Beverley Rach for design and production, and to Jane Butler and Sue Adams for their creative editorial assistance. I thank Errol Sharpe of Fernwood Publishing for his commitment to this project. I value his gentle way of working with authors and with texts.

In 1988 I submitted a version of this book to fulfill the requirements of my doctoral program. My aim was to construct an academic text which would be accessible to a non-academic audience. Bending the rules of thesis production required the courage and support of several people. I want to reiterate my deeply felt appreciation to all the persons acknowledged in the original book.

preamble

A: Fragments

Feminism is a politics. It is a politics directed at changing existing power relations between women and men in society. These power relations structure all areas of life, the family, education and welfare, the worlds of work and politics, culture and leisure. They determine who does what and for whom, what we are and what we might become (Weedon, 1987:1).

We know that knowledge is not something out there to be disseminated—and that politics is not confined to public, organized spheres of practice—but we've yet to develop academic forms which fully recognize the radical implications of a feminist critique (Rockhill, 1986:17).

I think that what we have to do, this we being located in individuals like myself within the apparatus of education, in part is to start examining where we are. How do our neutral, natural, universal and Obvious forms operate, what is their differential impact, how are we embodied in them, what do they encourage and what do they deny (Corrigan, 1984:21).

This is a story about beginnings and endings. It is a story about all that comes between beginnings and endings and all that comes before and after beginnings and endings. It is a story about some of what I have imagined, experienced and theorized and that which I might yet imagine, experience and theorize. In many ways it a story about me. Mostly, it is a story about social relations and how I and (some) others organize and construct our daily practices. In this sense, it is a story about relations of power. In another sense, it is about knowing, learning and observing, about how we observe, why, and for whom. In yet another sense, it is a love story about teachers and teaching, about thanks, about recognition, and about the subject of returning the self to the self, awake and undamaged. It is not the great awakening of which I speak, but rather, the everyday work of subjects who (care to) learn to awaken others gently, and with love. What else? The Beginning.

I began writing the stories which you are about to read in the spring of 1987 while I was a student in the department of sociology at the Ontario Institute for Studies in Education. My intent was to use these stories as the data for my doctoral dissertation. I decided to write about my experiences of abuse because I wanted to understand how my learning and knowing was shaped by that abuse. I was motivated by a desire to know how I had learned not to know something as significant as my own experiences of abuse.

I did not begin my doctoral program knowing that I would write a PhD thesis about my experiences of abuse. Rather, my intent was to study the experiences of battered women. During the years I was collecting data about battered women, I did not realize the contradiction in expecting them to share their stories with me while I remained silent about my own abuse. I did not perceive my silence as a contradiction, in part because I had buried my memories of abuse. At a more insidious level, I had learned to believe that my experiences were not important. What had happened to me, I thought, had absolutely nothing to do with my social history. For example, prior to writing my thesis I was unable to connect my fears of intimacy, writing, teaching, and speaking publicly to my experiences of abuse. I would learn through writing my thesis that I was unable to make this connection because I had not been taught to critique the world as it appeared to me. Instead, years of un-critical, rote learning had taught me how to not know.

I think a coalescence of several factors resulted in my learning to critique, how to know better about my experiences of abuse. Many of these factors are in the stories which make up this book. Some are implied rather than discussed. Importantly, I was able to begin the long process of learning to critique, specifically my experiences of abuse, because I was writing in an environment which I perceived as relatively safe. I learned to feel safe because of my work with students and teachers struggling with a variety of theoretical feminist perspectives. In this environment I was privileged to hear many women's stories of abuse. For the first time in my schooling experience I was studying with a large number of feminist scholars who valued women's stories, who offered me a caring, coherent, and universal theoretical analysis of, and alternative to, male-organized social practices. Of particular interest is the analysis of how knowledges are organized to differently benefit men and women. At the same time I was privileged to be working with a warm and caring dream therapist who taught me to re-connect with the self I had lost through abuse. Feeling safe in the context of this new way of knowing, I began to learn to write from a place of joy rather than from a place of dread and trepidation. Freed, I felt absolutely driven by a desire to develop research methods which would not violate the people with whom I was working. I think it was this combination of factors, and undoubtedly others, which enabled me to begin writing an autobiographical thesis. Nonetheless, I continued to worry about the problem of how to do research.

This problem is one which continues to plague me. However, learning to critique through autobiographical reflection and analysis is one means by which researchers, teachers and students can begin to know and examine the biases and assumptions which organize different ways of working. Such an approach is beneficial because it does not depend on an artificial separation of the personal and the public. Had I, at an early age, been taught autobiographical analysis as a way of learning to think and write critically, I might have been spared years of pain and silence.

My concern with research methods reached a crisis when I decided to shift from a study of women who had been battered to a study of my own experiences of abuse. From a place of self-exploration I knew that I did not want to fit my experiences into a traditional thesis form designed to omit subjectivity, emotion and feeling. Importantly, I felt I would violate myself if I were to speak about abuse in a detached objective, academic manner. Secondly, I had begun to suspect that there was a theoretical relationship between the kinds of fixed academic practices which I had been subjected to for most of my schooling experience and my inability to write or speak about abuse. For this reason, I decided I wanted to experiment with an alternative to the traditional thesis form. This decision, of course, depended largely on the support of a committee who were courageous enough to bend the rules.

With the support of my committee, I chose to write an autobiographical/theoretical/fictional analysis of my experiences of abuse. Theoretically, this approach is important because it enabled me to begin the process of healing through writing. It also provided a context within which I could critique where I am in the apparatus of education (Corrigan, 1984:21). Though Corrigan's statement is directed at male researchers who have not yet learned to examine their positions of power and authority, I think his words are equally applicable to women such as myself who are learning how to examine 'where we are not' in the educational apparatus.

I do not assume that the stories I construct constitute any form of the truth, though they are for me a 'kind' of truth. They do not constitute truth for two reasons. First, each writing produces differing and continuous theoretical understandings and analyses. Second, undoubtedly the people of whom I speak would tell another version of these stories. Because these stories are true only in so far as they reflect a perspective, I refer to them as fictional. In general, I think this distinction applies to all theoretical texts.

For reasons of privacy, I decided to re-name several people who appear in the text. In this sense, the people are fictional. In another sense, this remains the story of my life. I use fictional names, for the most part, to protect myself. I also do it to protect others. At no time did I write my stories for the purpose of hurting others. Rather, I wrote to reclaim my life.

The stories which I construct, as well as the three essays which I introduce in this work, are all discussed and analyzed in the context of letters I wrote to three fictional persons who in fact, constituted my thesis committee. The fictional names are significant for the following reasons. I chose the name Lily because I was profoundly inspired by my reading of Meigs' book *Lily Briscoe: A self-portrait: An autobiography* (1981). Reading this bolstered my desire to construct a self-portrait. I chose the name Andrew because of my love and respect for a dear friend's father, now deceased, whose name was Andrew. Virginia, of course, is in memory of Virginia Woolf who too was a survivor of sexual abuse. Importantly, each of these names in some way reminded me of the persons who formed my thesis committee. Given my learned and disrupted relationship to figures of authority, I found it helpful to create fictional names for the members of my committee because it enabled me to view them in a non-threatening, non-hierarchical way.

For the most part, I felt joy in the production of this work. In particular, I enjoyed writing letters. This enabled me to feel responsible for my assumptions and ideas. I felt too that my letters connected me to my committee in very real ways. Our correspondence provided me with a basis from which to think of my thesis as a collective dialogue. Responses to my work were key and often enabled me to dig further than I imagined I might. Never, for example, were my attempts at analysis and description responded to in a confrontational manner. Instead, responses to my work were insightful, questioning, and supportive.

In retrospect, I feel that our method of corresponding with one another, combined with regular meetings, enabled us to converse in a respectful manner about areas of concern, difference and agreement. From such a perspective, I was able to enjoy the work of producing a thesis, which all too often is done in stressful solitude. Because I felt empowered by my experience of producing an unusual work, I now question the theoretical validity of expecting students to produce (only) non-creative academic writing projects which actually work to reproduce illusions.

Theoretically, two factors are key to how I learned to write in the production of my thesis. Once I was freed to write the words "I was sexually abused as a child," I felt as if a shroud had been lifted from my body. In this lifting I learned that I could speak the unspeakable; there was, therefore, nothing imaginable which I could not express. And with the lifting of the shroud, I began to feel freed of an internalized authority, learned through my abuse. Freed, I could begin writing and thinking from my own perspective. This meant, of course, learning to see through the myriad of socially organized illusions which had initially taught me to reproduce my childhood abuse. In the process of reclaiming my own authority, I have begun to know the power of transgressing boundaries and limits. The data I present suggests the need for an academic reconsideration of writing and reading practices which work to keep relations of power and authority in place, thus hindering development of creative, non-rote schooling practices.

In the early stages of learning to critique socially organized illusions, I found it difficult to trust my own words or perspectives. I was like a child learning to read and write anew. For this reason, I very consciously borrowed the words of others. I chose them because they acted as a kind of view-finder for me. In other words, I used borrowed language to see through to my own experience, story, perspective. For this reason, I begin each chapter with quotes. And, though I use these quotes to get in touch with my own key words and concepts, I discovered how the words of others could help me learn the technique of critiquing. Thus, I began to work from a less defensive perspective than I had known previously. In part, this is because I began to learn about knowledge and ideologies as socially constructed and organized. Knowing this, I am inclined to spend less time defending my perspectives and more time working to develop creative perspectives. An analysis of the data used to organize this work suggests that my learning about knowledge as constructed is dependent on knowing the implications of my key words. I suggest, therefore, a need for safe learning environments where students of all ages can begin to know their key words. Without this knowledge rote learning is inevitable.

The learning which I describe and analyze is not peculiar to my way of learning, either as a woman or as a survivor of abuse. Rather, what I analyze herein is applicable to the experiences of many. I think, moreover, that educational theorists who have previously relied on explanations of learning and development drawn largely from male experience would benefit greatly from close scrutiny of stories such as those you are about to read. If, as reported in the work of Belenky et al. "38 percent of the women in schools and colleges and 65 percent of women contacted through the social agencies" (1986:58-59) have been subjected to incest, rape, or sexual seduction by a male in authority over them (these figures do not include the numbers of boys who too are abused) and if, in fact, abuse (or trauma) impedes how people learn and develop, as my stories suggest, then it is indeed time that teachers begin to re-examine teaching practices and researchers begin to re-examine the out-moded models of learning and development produced by theorists such as Perry (1970).

Lastly, it has been suggested that my work is not about feminist pedagogy. I have decided that I will not argue this point. Rather, I would like to share with you why I chose this title. I know that I could not have produced this book without the help of scholars learning to work from theoretical perspectives and teaching practices defined as feminist. Moreover, it was not accidental that I learned to feel safe enough to confront my experiences of abuse in an environment where scholars offered a universal and coherent analysis of, and alternative to, male-organized educational and social practices. I know that I could not have written my thesis without this analysis. Thus, I use the term feminist pedagogy to refer to the practices which enabled me to write this text. My aim is to illustrate why I think feminist practices are key for many, if not most, students.

Teacher: Imagine. How it feels to learn how to read, write and think when all you feel is badly about yourself. Imagine.

introduction

A: Subjects In/Formation: Problems and Perspectives

If our sexuality is the primary site of our oppression as women—what does it mean when we cannot talk about it in our work unless it is in terms of *those* women and children—out there—who are battered and abused (Rockhill, 1986:6-7)?

Based on our data, sexual abuse appears to be a shockingly common experience for women. In our sample of seventy-five women, 38 percent of the women in schools and colleges and 65 percent of women contacted through the social agencies told us that they had been subject to either incest, rape, or sexual seduction by a male in authority over them—fathers, uncles, teachers, doctors, clerics, bosses. Abuse was not limited to any... grouping of women . . . nor was it limited to any specific class, ethnic, or age group... (Belenky et al., 1986:58-59).

The central problem is this: How can the oppressed, as divided, unauthentic beings, participate in developing the pedagogy of their liberation? Only as they discover themselves to be hosts of the oppressor can they contribute to the midwifery of their liberating pedagogy. As long as they live in the duality in which to be is to be like, and

to be like is to be like the oppressor, this contribution is
impossible (Freire, 1970:33).

Dear Lily, Andrew and Virginia:

The purpose of this letter is to (formally) introduce you to the *subject matter* of my thesis, as well as to talk with you about how I understand myself as a *subject producing* this text. Within this discussion my aim is to share with you some of the assumptions which prompt me to write about the *subject* of feminist pedagogy rather than to write about battered women.

In the early stages of recognizing my abuse, I was shocked by the extent to which different forms of abuse had shaped my educational experience. I decided I could not write about how women's learning is affected by abuse without also examining how I had come to this realization in specific ways; from my experience of learning and writing about my abuse within the context of my academic studies, I was motivated to write about and develop further redressive pedagogical practices.

For a variety of reasons, I want to introduce this subject matter to you in the form of a letter. Of course, it is neither usual nor *obvious* (Corrigan, 1984) to write a thesis in the form of letters. My reasons for doing so are both simple and complex. Simply, I am writing to inform. Given the geographical distances between us, it is important that I keep you fully informed. More complexly, my decision to use a combination of forms, such as narrations and letters, comes from a desire to write in ways less defining and confining than the more usual and obvious ones. Inspired by the work of Rockhill, I am attempting to follow my heart and break out of the kinds of forms which can "limit, shape and even jeopardize a different kind of feminist work" (1986:3). Having decided to do this, I would ask that you read—differently—what I am writing: a way of reading described by Grumet as both close and distant (1981:211). Basically, my aim is to share with you my *developing* thesis, rather than present you with a completed work. Supporting Corrigan's (1984) concern with the operation of obvious forms, my intent is to construct an academic text somewhat different from the usual format.

Having made my decision to write in a not so obvious way, I do not assume that my decision will not intrude upon your work as supervisors. I am aware of some of the implications of my choices and how these choices might present problems for a committee working within an academic institution. Within this context, I recognize that my method of work might well be unacceptable. I am, of course, prepared and willing to consider your responses and suggestions. I will not, however, attempt to fit my subject into an *acceptable* form just for the purpose of getting it through. Because I care very much about this work I will no longer do it in a manner which is hurtful either to myself or to others.

My desire to work in a more positive, less hurtful way was affirmed recently in a letter from my dear friend Patsy, who wrote of her decision not to complete her thesis despite the fact that she had done most of the required work. I would like to share with you why, in the latter stages of her program, she decided not to complete it. She wrote:

> Studying Judaism ... did not allow me to view it through the eyes of Jewish women, except to a very limited extent. Herein lies the problem. I am in a Patriarchal structure writing about one of its religions. Being a woman and a non-Jew reduces my visibility even further. I am the Other writing as the Other. It is far too difficult. I have the feeling that I'm *Ghost Writing* my own work. I am the Ghost/Shadow using the male voice. There is no way around it. So I will opt out. I was naive in thinking that I had the inner reserves to get me through the Patriarchal maze. It is the structure, the way I must frame my work, and the knowledge that I must then **defend** it before a group of people who have no idea what I really think or feel which forces me to opt out (Campbell, 1987:1).

I wept when I read Patsy's letter. I wept for her, for myself, and for all the women I know who are struggling with the contradictions involved in reproducing the legitimized masculine perspectives. Patsy's choice, circumscribed by dominant educational practices, was to not subject herself to these dictates. She withdrew from the program. Thus, while Patsy has acted in a way which enables her to assume her own authority, she is nonetheless unable to complete a degree which she set out to attain, a degree for which she did most of the work.

Patsy's problem, of course, is not just Patsy's problem. It is part of a larger theoretical and methodological problem for women of how to locate our subjective, social selves in our research, writing, and teaching practices within institutions dedicated to what Smith refers to as a male mode of consciousness which *bifurcates* women's consciousness (1987:6-9). This is a problem, I suggest, which both female and male academics must address in order to develop new kinds of pedagogical practices and critical theories, which will better enable us to address the relationship of abuse, schooling practices and gender formation.

The problem of how abuse affects the learning of girls and women is, likewise, a problem of great importance. This week I read Fraser's (1987) memoir of incest and healing. I cried each time her words made me feel my anger, my fear, my pain and my own memories of abuse. In so many ways, her words reaffirm my choice to write about feminist pedagogies from my perspective as a survivor of incest. Written autobiographically, her words reach out to me, offering me support in my attempts to write from my perspective as an abuse survivor.

In reading her story, anger and determination again motivate me to understand and write about some of the ways in which abuse affects how I learn and develop, particularly in an academic context. Anger and determination also motivate me to write about the multitude of ways in which relations of power can work to produce the well-kept secret of male violence against women. It is a terrible violence. And, it is reproduced through schooling practices such as those experienced by Patsy which work only too well to reinforce feelings of fear, inadequacy and contempt—teaching us that it is not nice, not scholarly and certainly not scientific to speak of the personal in an academic context. These social practices work to bifurcate our consciousness, and in so doing, prevent us from actually talking about or knowing the illusions, assumptions and learned values which organize our everyday experiences. These forms work to silence women in many social contexts.

In resisting the kinds of academic practices which separate us from ourselves, from each other and from the knowledge of our ideological formations, my desire is to write a work in which I construct my subjective self in relation to the subject matter of feminist pedagogy. I begin from the assumption that feminist pedagogies are important for all students who suffer from any form of a bifurcated consciousness as a result of male violence. The intent of my writing, then, is to develop a theoretical perspective from which to analyze how specific relations of power work to organize my developing subjectivity, and how particular academic practices both hinder(ed) and aid(ed) my learning and development. How to access this knowledge for the purposes of contributing to the growing body of materials concerned with feminist pedagogy is central to this study. My aim is to pose a variety of questions while offering only fragmentary suggestions and multiple solutions.

But why, you ask, do I think it necessary to locate my subjective self in my academic practices? Well, as you know, I long ago set out to write a thesis about battered women. To this end, I collected a significant amount of data. From 1979 until the present, I read and collected every account I could find involving battered women. For years, I visited shelters throughout Canada, and I spent hours talking with battered women and their children, all of whom shared generously with me in the telling of their stories. In the early 1980s, I was trained as a shelter worker for the purpose of living, working, and doing research in a shelter for a period of four months. This enabled me to talk extensively with other workers about woman battering and about the problems involved in organizing women's shelters. For a brief time, I worked on the board of directors of a large Toronto shelter. Much of my leisure time was spent in intense discussion with women concerned with the problems and effects of male violence against women. This work now informs my teaching practices.

In my early attempts to write about battered women, each word I wrote felt like an insult to the women whose multiplicity of experiences I was privy. Frustrated, I attempted to write an "action-oriented" thesis for battered women in the Stanley and Wise (1983) sense. Not satisfied with this approach, I attempted to think through the methodological problems involved in working directly with shelter workers. From consultation with those directly involved with battered women, I hoped I might have better access to the *truth* of battered women's experiences. I assumed that because of their direct involvement with battered women the workers have a more truthful version of those women's experiences. I knew many workers had a highly sophisticated understanding of abused women. From this perspective, I imagined that the stories might bring me closer to the experiences of battered women than would my observations as an academic researcher.

Each attempt to research and write differently brought me back to the fact that I, or someone else, was describing the realities of others from our own perspectives. Not only was I describing the realities of battered women from my perspective, but I was doing so in the detached manner of an academic researcher. I felt like the ghost writer writing as the other: the objective researcher devoid of emotion and feeling (Campbell, 1987). Reproducing what I considered to be the norms of objective research, I wrote in a manner which rendered invisible the *actual* experiences of women. Adopting this approach meant that I was writing about *those women out there*. How different then, I wondered, was my feminist intent from that of the male perspectives I sought to go beyond? Struggling with this question, I knew that I must find out how I as 'the researcher' was located in the research process. In effect, I decided I could not begin to understand this problem until I could learn to examine the conditions of my own abuse.

Questions about what I know, about what I assume and about what I desire are often difficult for me to imagine and formulate. In part, this is so because sexual abuse taught me to live in the authority of an/other, my brother—a male—and in part because, as a woman, I was taught to live in and defer to the practices and authority of a society organized to benefit masculine interests (Smith, 1987). Thus, to ask questions which reflect my perspective as a woman means that I must first break through and understand, at one level, my experiences of abuse. At another level, I must break through and understand the social *illusions, practices* and *ideologies* created by social relations largely organized to legitimate men's interests. In such a context, it is difficult for me to un-learn sexual and social deference to male authorities, and then to work from an authority located in a conscious recognition of my own needs. I find it particularly difficult to un-learn deference to male authority within an academic context. This is so, I think, because of the abuse I experienced as a child, and because of my early and intense relationship to reading and schooling practices. In school I learned deeply to respect the written word, which is often constructed to reflect and support male interests. This learned respect works, I think, to make it difficult for me, for others, to see the (masculine) constructedness of the language available to me.

Why should these difficulties be surprising to me, I wonder? How was it, I now question, that I was able to learn to deconstruct the texts of others without learning to critique the texts which organize my everyday experiences? I remember well learning to systematically critique the work of others while doing my MA courses: I clearly recall being taught to recognize the implicit and explicit assumptions in a given work. What is more difficult is learning to critique the assumptions which organize my own perspectives. Until recently I was unable to examine why learning this is so difficult. I now think that it is very difficult for women to view the assumptions implicit and explicit in our works, within the context of male-organized social practices, because we are taught differently to reproduce male-constructed perspectives. Hence, to know our own subjective experience requires that we first learn and then unlearn the male-organization of all social perspectives.

In my opinion, men are taught to learn only the *obvious* and *legitimate* masculine perspectives. Difficult for men, I think, is learning that a masculine perspective is a socially constructed (not natural) and highly partial perspective from which it is difficult to understand the social and political production of gender differences. Thus, because a male perspective—that men have certain rights on the basis of gender (*Masculinity as Right*, Corrigan, 1987)—is adopted and sustained by both women and men, it should not be surprising to discover that I, and others, find it difficult to name our needs or to talk about the ways in which we are constructed and organized into particular gendered positions. Whether masculine or feminine, it is difficult to see the frameworks which organize us differently unless, of course, we are taught to approach these frameworks critically.

Prior to my decision to change my thesis focus, I had not written about my experiences of abuse. Simply, I did not assume there to be a connection between my interest in battered women and my experience of abuse. I assumed I could ask women to tell me their stories of abuse, and I could write these stories without ever telling mine. At one level, I feared that I would not be taken seriously if I were to tell my story. And even if I were taken seriously, I worried that I would be judged and condemned. Only too well do I know the glazed eyes, shuffling feet and uncomfortable reactions when people begin to talk about that which is considered private and therefore not acceptable for public discourse. Sometimes my discussions of battered women produce this kind of discomfort, especially when presented in an academic context.

At another level, I did not actually consider my experience to be significant, certainly not with respect to my academic work. My experience, I thought, was *just* one factor in my social history and not necessarily an important one. From such a perspective, how could I possibly take seriously the stories of other women? Educational practices had taught me well not to discuss or conceptualize that which appears socially unacceptable and theoretically insignificant.

The question of how particular kinds of social experiences come to be identified as social problems is important for many researchers. Only recently, for example, are educational researchers beginning to address and document the effects of sexual, mental, and physical abuse which women may experience through educational practices (Belenky et al., 1986; McMahon, 1986; McIntyre, 1986; Rockhill, 1986, 1987). The recent work of Rockhill is an excellent example of one researcher's attempt to break through the traditional boundaries of academic *correctness* for the purpose of documenting, analyzing, and theorizing male abuse on the basis of personal experience.

The difficulties involved in this kind of work are immense. Not only does Rockhill's work demand that she confront the ghosts of her past, but that she, like other scholars who take up this kind of work, go beyond her preconceived notions of what constitutes *serious academic work*. And this kind of confrontation is minor to that which she may later confront, when her work is entered into a larger social discourse: to an audience which may or may not receive her work favourably or, perhaps more importantly, may not take seriously her attempts to theorize subject matters only recently articulated. A significant number of scholars, however, are beginning to take up this kind of work, from a variety of feminist perspectives.

For example, a recent study by Belenky et al. documents the alarming fact "that among college women, approximately one out of five women described a history of childhood incest." Among less privileged social groups this study indicates that "almost one out of every two women reported a history of incest"(1986:59). These numbers, also reported in the work of Guberman and Wolfe (1985), indicate a serious social problem. Women of all races and classes are and can be abused. Not acknowledged in most theories of learning, nor openly discussed in most educational institutions, is how male abuse is a significant, but invisible, aspect of women's educational experience. Developmentally, male abuse is a highly ignored sociological variable. I will suggest how the inclusion of this variable indicates a need to rethink and re-analyze the political implications of current pedagogical practices.

Less explicitly, the relationship of abuse to women's education is being analyzed in autobiographical accounts (see, for example, Fraser, 1987 and Spring, 1987). From a focus on their experiences of incest, Fraser and Spring indirectly demonstrate how incest adversely shaped their educational experiences. Other forms of abuse, such as sexual harassment in the workplace, are documented (see, for example, Backhouse and Cohen, 1978 and McIntyre, 1986). These are important accounts because they show how women's fear of male abuse, even in the absence of physical abuse, can work to adversely affect women's schooling experiences. Women's everyday fear of rape works, I suggest, in a similar manner.

While an increasing number of texts document and analyze the prevalence and wide ranging practices of abuse against women (Pizzey, 1974; MacLeod, 1980; Brookes, 1982; Dobash and Dobash, 1979; Kincaid, 1982; Wilson, 1983; Beaudry, 1985; Guberman and Wolfe, 1985; Okum, 1986; Vallee, 1986; Rockhill, 1986), few accounts explicitly examine and analyze, from a personal perspective, the relationship of women's abuse to schooling practices.

From my perspective as an abuse survivor, I intend to examine the ways in which abuse affects all aspects of my social experience, in particular my identity, my learning, my development. I intend to examine how this learning and development was disrupted by an abuse which taught me a perspective and authority not my own. Central to this study is an analysis of how knowledge is socially organized. Based on the data of my thesis, I will analyze how schooling practices, like practices of male abuse, work to silence women. I think it horrifically ironic that I now understand the implications of abuse on my learning and development in a context in which I was originally taught not to see, and which prevented me from knowing, and naming, my abuse. To begin to resist this oppression is to begin redefining the very frameworks of our oppression.

Love and Solidarity.

chapter one

A: Breaking the Silence

This is an invitation to share in a moment of inquiry about writing, history, and sexual difference and to witness my attempt to write from — to speak with — desire in and about a search for a way to create a living language within which I can recognize and create my self (McMahon, 1986:1).

My mother believes that what you save from the past is mostly a matter of choice (Atwood, 1983:16).

For years, I did not think of my situation as abusive — then one day I did and it's made all the difference to me (Rockhill, 1987:34).

The experiences which I describe and analyze in Chapter 1 all relate in some way to the fact that I was sexually abused as a child. This abuse, I now realize, shaped and organized my developing subjectivity. Inspired by the autobiographical work of Grumet (1981), my aim in Chapter 1 is to reconceptualize and reclaim aspects of my social history through narration, reflection and analysis. Through memory-work (Haug et al., 1987:14), my intent is to reconstruct, analyze, theorize and re-learn particular social experiences which I define as educational. My aim is to identify in these stories the dominant social practices which organized much of my learning, and to explicate what it means for me to talk about knowledge as socially constructed.

*Until quite recently, I was unable to write the words, I was sexually abused as a child. Deeply attached to words through my love of language, not being able to write these particular words was for me a problem. Not being able to write these words meant that I continued to be controlled at some level by a past that I wanted to erase. Not being able to write these words meant that I was controlled by feelings of shame, feelings which continued to shape my experiences, reminding me that I was not quite right. Sensing that my experience of abuse was not a safe topic for public discourse (I should keep it secret), I internalized and made **natural** the feelings of shame.*

Internalized, these feelings controlled me in a particular manner. In a rather strange way, I was able to pretend normality: I had not been abused. More bizarrely, I felt captive to feelings of specialness (that of not being normal). In effect, these illusions worked to separate me both from myself and from others. In narrating my experiences, I am beginning the process of saying NO to my illusions. In this NO, a NO denied me as a child, I am reclaiming and (re)cognizing an authority long ago stolen from me through sexual abuse. In this manner, Chapter 1 is more than an introduction and more than an exercise. It is an important social beginning; a subject in formation. Key to this (re)formation is my attempt to connect this process to an examination of how I understand and use the term 'feminist pedagogy'.

Dear Lily, Andrew and Virginia:

I am an Incest Survivor. I was sexually abused as a child. Sexual abuse shaped and seriously damaged my life. For many reasons it is difficult for me to understand the ongoing effects of this abuse in my adult life. Only recently am I beginning to understand how my choices are shaped by a past of which I am not fully cognizant. In part, this understanding is related to my decision to write about the abuse I suffered as a child. It was not, however, until the latter stages of my PhD work that I was able to write or talk about the abuses which organized many of my choices. This inability to name key life experiences is significant in view of the fact that I have researched male violence against women for a number of years. The question of how I was able to write about violence in the lives of battered women without writing about the violences in my own is key to the work you are reading. It is this question which, in fact, provoked me to shift my focus from the subject of battered women to the subject of how forms of abuse shape and influence how I learn and develop. As a consequence of this shift, I have begun to examine how specific feminist practices enable me to read and write beyond experiences of abuse. At the same time, this shift is enabling me to write beyond some of the limitations of academic practices which taught me to produce and reproduce social illusions.

I learned early and well how to produce social illusions in a schooling context. This is not a mysterious or difficult process. Quite clearly those who taught me to read and write also taught me that it was not safe to write about matters which would make either them or me uncomfortable in a classroom context. Stories which never addressed issues such as sexual abuse reinforced this teaching. Hence I, like others, learned early to divide my self and my world into categories such as private and public, practice and theory, good and bad. Once this method of learning was internalized, it was easy for me to assume that my experience of abuse was neither important nor appropriate. Thus, as a child being taught to read, write, and talk, I learned that abuse was an unacceptable topic for discussion. I learned that some topics are good and that some are bad. I concluded, therefore, that if the subject matter was unworthy of discussion, then I too must be unworthy. Hence, I must be silent. How could I know otherwise?

I am discovering that this way of learning is even more firmly entrenched in the organization of advanced academic practices. There are, of course, individual and collective exceptions. For example, at the collective level, there is an emerging and varied feminist, Marxist, and critical scholarship which is intended to critique relations of power. In keeping with what I perceive to be the spirit of this work, I have organized my text as a series of letters and stories within which I will examine and reconstruct some of the abusive practices which prevented me from knowing myself as an abused child and woman.

The following story was written with considerable ease, on one hand, and, on the other, with discomfort. Words flowed once I allowed myself to return to a past I had been taught to forget. Each memory, however, produced yet another memory. Some of them I chose not to describe, in part for my own protection and safety, and in part because I do not think they are key. I chose, however, to begin this work with the following story because it was from this perspective that I first began to disentangle myself from specific kinds of abuse.

B: Breaking the Sequence

> It is difficult, but not impossible to disentangle ourselves from the culture in which we have been formed. Autobiography provides the possibility of reconstruction (Grumet, 1981:336).

To ascertain where one is, when one is, one must locate the past. Location means identification and bracketing the past. Bracketing means looking at what is not ordinarily seen, at what is taken-for-granted, hence loosening oneself from it. As the past becomes present, the present is revealed. So it is we aim at freedom from the past, freedom in the present. Such objectives require entrance into the past as a first step (Pinar, 1976:56).

I was born in a small *university town* in rural New Brunswick. Our sprawling two-storey white farm house sat at the edge of town, bordered on one side by a working farm. The wonderful smells associated with the farm still linger with me. On the other side of our family property was a small urban-like street peppered with older, freshly-painted houses. Sometimes I played with the children who lived in these houses. Often I played alone. I loved the musty smelling attic of our house. I seldom ventured into the damp, dark basement except when I was told to fetch potatoes and apples from the old wooden bins. That old house sits, yet, on the edge of a small New Brunswick town.

Our family property consisted of several unfarmed acres. Neighbours farmed our corn fields in the summer. My parents were not farmers. Despite family responsibility for a large apple orchard and a very large summer garden, along with chickens and other small animals, my parents were considered town folks. In practice, Mom taught me the secrets of the ocean. She took me there to play. Dad taught me the secrets of the land and the woods. In summer, I learned how to graft apple trees, pick potato bugs and weed a garden. In the late winter I learned, among other things, how to sugar maple trees and how to rid the wild rabbits of ear mites. More than my father, my mother was privileged materially by an upper-class background. In practice, both my parents worked. My mother, Alese, worked at home raising five children - Robbie, Mark, myself, Peter, and Ricky. My father, Nathan, worked in the woods. He managed the work of other men. In spirit, my mother was an artist, my father a writer. I am told that my mother's third pregnancy was fraught with difficulty. She wanted a girl. My birth was a miracle, they say.

At the centre of our family property was a pond. In winter the pond was a skating rink. In summer it was a place to be avoided, though many secret summer hours were spent rafting on what I came to think of as the "polio" pond. Sitting at the edge of the swampy pond, I sometimes observed the New Brunswick herons flying overhead. I would listen to the croaking frogs or watch with awe the dragonflies as they buzzed about my head. My younger brother told me that dragonflies would sew up my mouth if I talked too much. His words worried me. At the rear of our property was a wooded area. In what seemed like the centre of the wooded area there was a clearing. Through this ran a trickling brook. It was a magic place. Many a summer moment was spent with my feet in the brook. Here, I felt lovely and free. Stretching away from the wooded area were fields of corn. Raspberry and blueberry bushes grew along the fences bordering the corn fields, as did hollyhocks and morning glories. The fences connected the back of the property with the old barns leaning upright just behind our home, some distance from the pond.

The view from the front of our property was eerie and different from the view at the back. The marshes of New Brunswick are flat and desolate. At the same time, the marshes are expansive and beautiful, reaching out to the wildness of the high tides of the Bay of Fundy. Oftentimes we swam in the nearby ocean. I liked to gaze out at the marshes, remembering warm sands, the taste of dulse and the feel of early morning fogs. From the upstairs bedroom of our house I could see the road to Nova Scotia between the red marsh mud and the salt water dykes. The view was best in early spring and late fall, when the trees were bare. In the distance I could see the Nova Scotia border. At least I imagined I could. My view was only slightly obstructed by the intrusion of large radio towers. At night the towers shone brightly in the darkness of the marshes. I liked watching the tall radio towers because they connected me, or so I thought, to the rest of the world.

Fall is my favourite season in New Brunswick. Walking from my home to the centre of town took about twenty minutes. The walk to town and back is something I remember well. I felt good as I swished through the fallen leaves. In the near distance, church bells sounded with regularity. I imagined dancing through the leaves. I loved the sounds and smells. The smell of burning wood from nearby homes warmed me inside as I walked through the sunny, often chilly, air. Back and forth from home to town I walked through the fall, fearing little.

Saturdays were particularly happy days. Early Saturday morning, Dad cooked breakfast on the old wood stove. While he worked, he talked with us. I remember feeling grown-up. It was the way in which he asked questions, I think. Mom was often too tired to ask questions. And usually too tired to listen. The work of five children, the work of a home, the care of Dad, took all her energy. Saturday was also movie day. For ten cents I was occasionally granted two hours of magic of a different order. There were no televisions then. Even more important than my time at the movie theatre was the time I spent in the children's library, located in the basement of the university library. On Saturday mornings, I borrowed books. It was here that I learned to read and write long before I went to school. It was here that I learned to believe in the power of words as I listened with awe to wonderful story-tellers. Best of all, I was free to wander through the old university library with its spiral staircases, imagining, as I quietly moved in and around the stacks of books, that I would one day read all those books. I imagined that I would be a teacher, just like Mrs. Patterson, my grade one teacher. Living in a small, supposedly safe community meant that I was allowed to roam about freely at a very early age, especially on Saturdays, when my parents were busied by weekend chores.

Between the library and the movie theatre was a small duck pond. It sat in front of the winter sledding hill from which, if I listened carefully, I could hear the sound of music from the nearby opera house. These were sites of pleasure. The sloping park area which housed the pond and the hill provided a natural division between the town and the university. I liked to walk through the park in the fall. Here I felt the excitement of the incoming university students. I didn't, of course, know them then as university students. I knew only the sense of excitement and colour which accompanied their movements. This excitement matched my childhood anticipation of more to come as my mother prepared my four brothers and me for yet another school year. I remember most the new pencil cases and the smell of new paper. Dad paid for them, or so we pretended. My memories of the duck pond, Saturdays, schools, libraries, theatres, music, books, fall, Mom and Dad, are inextricable.

Then everything changed although I am told otherwise. Inside I was different, I was changed, yet I had neither the words nor the courage to speak my difference. My secret was terrible and dark. No one understood why I began to wet my bed at night. No one understood why I wanted to spend weekends at my friend Margaret's farm, on the other side of town. I remember not smiling. My parents remember otherwise. Absolutely no one seemed to notice I was different. My parents' friends commented on my beauty. But being lovely on the outside didn't matter at all to me. My insides were too troubled. My parents remember that I talked a lot. I remember silence. I expect both memories are important. Sometimes talking is a way of forgetting. I remember the headaches. I remember the sleepless nights. I remember the nightmares: men who wanted to kill me chased me through darkened streets. I remember crying in the night. I found it difficult to hear Mrs. Patterson when she spoke in the classroom. I felt as if she were speaking from beneath tumbling water, or from the end of a long tunnel. She assumed I was daydreaming. I stopped imagining that I might one day be a teacher. Teachers were required to stand up in front of their students. I knew I wouldn't be able to stand up in front of people and talk. Not me. Everyone would know, I thought. No longer did my imagination dance me through the leaves. The sound of ringing church bells irritated me. Mostly I felt ashamed, different. I am an incest survivor. I was changed.

My family emigrated to New Zealand just shortly before my twelfth birthday. Except for my older brother. He went away to an Upper Canadian university. I thought I might now feel safe. But I didn't. Inside I was still afraid. I wanted to tell my parents. I wanted to tell someone why I was different. Who would believe me? He had said it was my fault. He had told me that our parents would be angry with me. I believed him. It was easier in New Zealand. For a while. In a way, school was easier. Reading was a pleasure which enabled me to escape, when I needed to, from myself and from others. Teachers reported me a good student. Being a good student was easy. It was easy, that is, until I was expected to stand up or speak in front of my classmates. This was painful. Afraid, I would vacate my body so as not to remember.

Still, living in New Zealand was easier. There were the rivers, the ocean and the incredibly beautiful countryside. I felt safer with my older brother away at university in Canada. I remember laughing again. I recall hearing the teacher's voice. I felt safer, that is, until the night my mother was brutally raped as she walked home alone from a neighbourhood party. Seeing her tortured body early that morning and hearing her anguish as she later endured the brutal questioning and blaming by my father and the police was more than I (or she) could bear.

In my memory, the subsequent denial of my mother's abuse ultimately froze my own secret into a silence from which I was unable to escape for a very long time. The events of that night were not mentioned for many years. In this silencing I, like my mother, was ruled by unspoken fear and trauma. In time we would both forget, on a conscious level, why we were terrified to be alone. Consciously, I wanted to be normal, to have a *normal* mother. In this desire I learned to distrust and reject my mother, myself, and the fears which shaped us differently. Until the night of her rape, I had managed to survive my own terrible secret. Burdened by yet another secret, I learned to fear madness. Who would take care of me? My mother? My father, who had chastised and judged my mother? Men, who would rape me? I feared the terrible rage inside me. I worked to control it. At the age of thirteen, unable to speak the words which might free me, I remember wanting to die. Twice that year I was hit by a car. Each time they said it was an accident. I thought so too.

Returning to Canada with my mother and my younger brothers, without my father, who viewed New Zealand as his new home, was excruciatingly difficult. He had been a protector of sorts. In my memory, he left us. In fact, in a way, he did. He stopped sending money. My mother took on a second job and began to absent herself even more in overwork and alcohol. I remember feeling responsible for her. She didn't, of course, need me. I needed her. But I didn't know that then. I also needed my father. But I didn't know that then, either. I've never really forgiven my father. Nor did he forgive me for not writing to him. I couldn't tell him about the physical pain I experienced when I attempted to write. I stopped writing. So did he.

It was agonizing to write with a war going on inside of me. Fear, anger, and the knowledge of something else ate away at my insides. Doctors called it ulcers. People continued to speak of my outside beauty. I resented my developing body. It made me feel obvious, which made me more anxious. I wanted only to hide. On the outside, life continued as usual. I worked. I studied. The work was easy. Often I forgot what I learned. I needed so desperately to forget. My hours were filled with part-time jobs, people who didn't matter to me and dates I can't remember. I never told. *What was there to tell?* In classrooms, movies, work places, Girl Guide halls, churches, restaurants, or in discussions with friends and family, no one spoke of a shame like mine. I assumed there was nothing to say. Classmates voted me beauty queen and cheerleader. The *honour* terrified me. Contradictorily, while seeking affirmation, I wanted to escape. I felt haunted. I began to actively forget. I sought refuge in marriage, a young husband and a baby. Nothing produced the peace I so desperately sought. At the age of nineteen I decided to end my life. It was just too painful. The doctor who sewed up my razor-slit arms listened. I told only enough to provide a reason for my suicide attempt. His way of questioning didn't allow me to trust that I could safely tell my whole story. I probably couldn't. It took me many more years to write **I am an incest survivor**. Amnesia persists. I still vacate my body when I am afraid. The ulcers are gone, however, and the war is lessening.

I remember little about my early schooling experiences. I do remember feeling lonely and different, older than my friends and classmates. Teachers, I recall, reacted to me in two ways: because of my reading ability, I was occasionally moved to an accelerated class; other times, teachers reported that I was not working to my potential. Mostly, I remember not wanting to be in the classroom, but contradictorily, I sometimes longed for its safety. Emotional and actual absences from school were common for me. My love of reading continued. One cold day in January, grade eleven, I remember, I decided to leave school. In actual fact, I didn't decide. I thought I was pregnant. I wasn't. But I didn't return. I imagined that working might be easier. When it wasn't, I imagined marriage and babies. Nothing helped me escape myself, except perhaps my decision to die. This was the choice which finally empowered me to begin my long journey back, and ahead.

A brief encounter with a Freudian therapist enabled me to examine some aspects of the violence I had endured as an incest victim. For six months I sat in the office of a Dr. Brown and cried. In the silences between my tears, I could name only the shame and pain I felt. I could not name the abuse. Nonetheless, crying energized me. Energized, I decided to complete my high school education despite objections from my male partner, who felt threatened by this decision. His lack of support was manifested in his refusal to do child care so that I might study. In time, I ended my analysis, my marriage, and I entered the labour market as a relatively unskilled, underpaid worker and single parent of two growing boys. I recall thinking that I parented well. Sean and Ken were my reason for living. Then. Much of those years, too, is absent from my memory. I recall having no time to read or study. Somewhere in all of this I remarried and divorced again. I needed men. Then. It was through men that I defined myself. In sexual relations, I allowed men to possess me. Although not always, I recall.

Two years of intense therapy with a kind and gentle therapist and ten years of not always satisfactory work prompted me to take up my formal education again. Encouraged by Peter, and a dear priest friend, Augusto, I entered university for the first time. My original plan was to become a social worker or possibly a therapist, like Peter. Instead, I chose to major in religious studies. These were exciting and fearful years for me: exciting because I loved learning with others with whom I could identify; fearful, because I found it excruciatingly painful to write essays. I feared also speaking in groups of more than three. I did not connect these fears with the trauma of my childhood. Gently, Peter awakened in me a self that I'd forgotten. It was this work with Peter and my friendship with Augusto which enabled me to begin the work of healing. In their differing ways, they taught me that it was possible to reclaim my sexuality and my spirituality. Only later would I reclaim ways of learning. These reclaimings continue. Essay writing remains a problem.

I remember well my first years at university. Jennifer and Rosemary suffered with me my inability to write papers. Only later would I know this as related to abuse. Jennifer's and Rosemary's support enabled me to survive the system. Central to their love for me was the childcare which they so willingly offered. Sean and Ken speak happily of this time. In this friendship with Jennifer and Rosemary I began to know and to reclaim aspects of my womanness previously lost to me through abuse. I began to know differently my absent mother. Later I would know better my absent father. I remember three kind, excellent teachers, Sam, Louis and Paul. I think of them as mentors who guided and inspired me through a very demanding interdisciplinary undergraduate program. An introduction to a Marxist perspective turned my world upside-down, and the beginnings of feminist work turned me inside-out. Though unable to write an essay without incredible anxiety, I nonetheless remember these years with pleasure.

Enthused and energized by new perspectives from which to view the world, I chose (or so I thought) to marry again. I completed my undergraduate work in religious studies, gave birth to my daughter Sarah, became a faculty wife, identified myself as a radical feminist, *followed* my partner to the east coast and took up graduate work in an anthropology department in the community in which we lived. At the same time, I began a two-year period of intense work in a women's consciousness-raising group. This deeply affected me and the scholarly work I was attempting to do. More connected to women, and women's interests, I began to critique every aspect of my existence. Curiously, even in the safety of our group, I did not talk or write about the abuse I had endured as a child. The group, however, proved to be a base from which I began to see alternatives in the areas of both relationships and academic practices. In the safety of this group, I began to voice my fear of writing and of speaking in academic ways.

Speaking about incest is almost as difficult as learning to speak about academic oppression. Like many women scholars I know, I sensed and sometimes knew that male teachers treated female students differently than they did male students. Hence, I learned to resent and resist the privileges generally accorded male students. Anger empowered me to learn with renewed vigour. Fears of essay writing began to lessen. Academically, I did well in the field of anthropology. Life had taught me well how to be an observer. With the help of an important male mentor, I learned better to read and critique the work of others. Feeling safe enough to critique the work which *I* produced came much later. Rarely did I allow myself to imagine how far I might proceed with a formal education. I didn't trust yet that I could do this work.

Despite an abundance of fears, I completed my MA work. This work was difficult and challenging. I was challenged by the immense responsibility of understanding the experiences of battered women. This was made particularly difficult by the fact that I was examining male violence against women in an all-male department. Naively, I assumed I could write about battered women in this all-male department whose members were unversed in feminist scholarship. In the last year of my two-year MA program, I was harassed by a member of this department. From his perspective, my thesis topic was *too sensitive an issue* to constitute serious academic work. Despite his abuse and the subsequent fear which his abuse evoked in me, I managed to complete the work of my thesis. However, having begun to doubt even more the validity of my research, I was shocked when I received a Fellowship to continue this work.

In the safety of a new university setting, I began to confront a problem I had discovered in the work of my MA thesis. I first identified this as a problem of how to put myself, as a woman and researcher, into the text; how does one do research involving human subjects without making those people into objects, either in the research or writing process. When writing my thesis, I was frustrated by my inability to capture the complexities of the women's lives I was attempting to describe. The case histories I constructed appeared shallow in comparison with what I had come to know in my work with battered women. Further, I was frustrated by my inability to use and devise theory without overlaying the data with explanations which removed me from the everyday lives of battered women. Driven by a desire to do research differently, I struggled with this problem while completing the requirements of the program.

Motivated by readings undertaken outside the context of my formal studies, I began to suspect that my personal research problem was perhaps a universal one which could be addressed only among academics committed to gender issues. For this reason, I chose to leave midstream my studies in anthropology. My colleagues were supportive of my decision to work with scholars cognizant of feminist scholarship. At this time, I seriously considered leaving academe altogether, doubting less that I could do the work and more whether I would ever be able to address my concerns and questions in any formal academic setting.

Choosing to leave a program mid-stream was tough. Even tougher was finding an alternative place to study. The change meant that amidst an important, but slowly disintegrating marital relationship, I had to shift schools, move myself and my young daughter from one province to another, and begin my PhD course work. I had to complete an additional ten PhD courses and begin anew the study of another discipline. My decision to make this change was inspired by some other graduate students and a faculty member who were excited by the work they were doing in the areas of gender, race and class. The chair of the department suggested that I might hasten completion of my studies by writing course papers which would be the chapters of my thesis. With the exception of one paper, I did this.

Leaving a discipline which did not meet my immediate and long term needs meant that I found not one, but many, mentors. In this new environment I experienced the joy of working with students and teachers addressing explicitly, from a feminist perspective, the issues of concern to me in my study of battered women. I began at this point to better understand that learning does not occur separate from everyday experience. In other words, I began to know more consciously theory as connected to practice. The excitement and fear I felt as a result of this new way of learning prompted me to enter another two years of intense therapy. This work with an analyst committed to dream therapy, enabled me to begin learning about myself and about new ways of learning. My nightmares lessened. I began to trust my body. This trust is important for incest survivors. It was this combination of immersion in feminist scholarship and dream therapy which taught me to imagine new ways of doing academic research. Throughout this time I continued to believe I was writing a thesis about battered women.

I first suspected that I was not writing the thesis I thought I was writing when engaged in producing a formal thesis proposal. After four attempts to convince myself and my committee that I was writing about battered women, I wrote for the very first time the words which would alter dramatically my identity as a woman and a scholar. In writing the words **I was sexually abused as a child**, I was both thrown into turmoil and energized by the freedom of putting these words to paper, although at the time I did not understand why or how. Energized, I applied and was accepted for a teaching position in the department of sociology at Memorial University of Newfoundland.

Until I wrote the words and began in earnest the process of freeing myself from my *silence*, I had not imagined that I could teach. My fears were simply too acute. I knew I could not stand in front of others and do the work of teaching. My fear had rendered me powerless. Nonetheless, I continued to prepare myself for this work. In this sense, I worked continuously to reclaim aspects of myself not located in silence. Key to this reclaiming project was my decision to analyze my abuse through writing. The effects of this analysis, however, cannot be understood apart from the social relations and practices which allowed me to feel safe enough to confront my fears and do the work. In and through this method of learning to identify myself through writing, I am also learning about the need for changed pedagogical practices. From my perspective of gender analysis, I have begun to understand how abuse continues to inform my developing subjectivity. I am discovering the extent to which all women are victims of male violence. It is this knowledge which prompted me to further shift the focus of my thesis. I decided finally that I could not justifiably write about battered women without writing about how I am coming to know my social self, a self that was abused. This text, then, became an exercise in methodology (of the therapeutic kind).

C: Re-Visioning the Past

What's the difference between vision and a vision? The former relates to something it's assumed you've seen, the latter to something it's assumed you haven't. Language is not always dependable either (Atwood, 1983:61).

As we analyze narrative we reveal interests and biases we rarely see . . . . This is the second phase of reconceptualizing that illuminates the ways we organize and interpret our experiences by framing these choices in an aesthetic object, the autobiography (Grumet, 1981:13).

If therefore a given experience is possible, it is also subject to universalization (Haug et al., 1987:44).

I remember little about the sexual abuse I suffered as a child. Mostly, I remember fear. I know that my life was changed. I don't remember penetration. But I am not sure. I remember one event more fearful than the others. I recall moments of wanting to escape. I recall terror. Mostly, I remember terror. I remember not wanting to be left alone with my brother. I have vivid memories of hours spent away from home in the company of my friend Margaret, whose parents kindly welcomed and accepted me into their home, where I felt safe. Mostly, I remember feelings. I remember feeling out-of-control, afraid (of him), unable to breathe, to speak, unable to remember, afraid to face people. Even now these feelings return when I am afraid. I remember worrying that it might be my fault. I remember thinking my father was mean with Robbie. Mom told me that my father was mean to Robbie because he reminded him of her first husband. I remember well the respect which Robbie, who was eight years older than me, earned in school, where he always excelled. This respect made it difficult for me to take seriously my memory and experience of abuse.

What I do remember most about Robbie is locked in body memories which I carry as tension in my body. In learning, through abuse, not to trust my body, I also learned not to trust what I know. Not trusting what I know made it difficult to talk with others about my early experiences of abuse. Shame and doubt silenced me. Unable to name the shame located in deep body memories, I spent most of my early work in therapy trying to understand secondary symptoms rather than primary experiences.

In retrospect, I'm not certain that large numbers of men, or women for that matter, want to hear my story or the stories of other victims of abuse. The taboos are so firmly entrenched. Similarly, I'm not certain my parents wanted to hear my story. They were shocked when in later years I told them. They never again inquired. Only once did my mother speak openly about being raped. Too pained by her violent memories, she finds it difficult to affirm either of our experiences. My parents' ongoing silence about abuse also worked to silence me for quite some time. These responses teach us much about silence and repression and their effectiveness in reinforcing shame and doubt. My grandmother's stony response to my first divorce worked on me in much the same manner. Such responses taught me to hide from myself, from others, that which I came to know as socially unacceptable.

I have not confronted my brother Robbie. I am afraid to, because I fear he will deny the abuse. I also fear hurting him. When only a child, I was taught to respect Robbie. When grown, I learned to respect how he lives his adult life. But I shall, when I am able. I need to know why he thought it was permissible to abuse me. For too long I've excused him. He was young. He didn't know any better. He is a good family man. He is an important man. His work is important. I just imagined the whole experience. In excusing him, I deny my experiences. And I deny my body.

A denial of body is an ever-changing and recurring theme in my stories. It has many shapes and forms. Ambiguous, for example, is my love of school. As a young woman, I both loved and dreaded schools. At one level, schooling represented safety. At school I was away from home, away from my brother. Schools were safe places where I could lose myself in the reading of texts. I did not think then about the difficulties of locating my female self in texts which describe and reflect male interest and experience. Schools were also places of dread. Someone might discover my secret. Standing up always meant that I might be noticed. Writing, too, meant that I might be noticed. Like speaking, writing was painful. I felt buried by fears, pain and a desire to tell. Hiding behind my pain, in a society which condones male abuse of women, I found it difficult to either write or speak from my own perspective. Of the impersonal, I spoke more easily.

In not writing or speaking about my abuse, I learned to relegate my authority to others: to men, or to any authority figure. This relegation of authority became a fixed part of my identity in my thirteenth year, when I was forced to contend with my visibly developing female body, my desires, my own previous sexual abuse, my mother's abuse, my fears, my parents' separation, and the silences I worked to keep under control. At the age of thirteen I relinquished my own authority. Silent, I felt strangled by the fears and secrets which simmered inside of me. I am no longer surprised that I have difficulty breathing when afraid. How abuse survivors lose access to our own authority is well documented in the work of Rockhill, who writes about the effects of her abuse:

> I felt trapped. I had to be totally inside his subjectivity, or I feared I would go mad. In the process, I lost access to my own experience, feelings, viewpoint. I had learned to do this as a child — to render myself invisible by vacating my body. The sensation was one of taking up no space, doing all that I could not to be noticed, becoming the perfect observer (1986:26).

As a victim of abuse, I became the perfect observer. In retrospect, it is not surprising that I was attracted to the academic study of anthropology: it was a safe place from which to observe the lives of anyone other than myself. In leaving anthropology, I began to create a space in which I could confront the ghosts of my past, a past which I sought to make visible through writing.

For many years prior to this confrontation, I related to women and men from a sexually abused body which needed to be invisible. Vacating my body was an important means of survival. In shutting out feeling and emotion, I learned well to live in my head, where I imagined that I could ignore the fears experienced only at the level of body. Living in my head meant I had little access to body information. Living in my head meant learning to *cope* with a male-organized world. Living in my head now means that I sometimes find confrontation difficult.

To repress my feelings of discomfort, I learned a variety of coping strategies. For example, I learned that food could check energy. I learned it was easier to suppress my fears when feeling full or dull. Dullness removed me from accountability and responsibility. This worked to quiet me, keeping in check my desire to know and receive pleasure. I learned, too, that one way of accessing space is to take it up in body weight. Sometimes fatness, like thinness, works to keep people at a distance. Through a fear of anger, I learned to deny my emotional and bodily responses. I came to welcome and fear shifts in energy. Such shifts, I discovered, could precede the end of something or alternately, the beginning of something. Both situations were fearful. Through practice, I learned to cope by quickly retreating into the head space where a rational, unconnected masculine voice allowed me to excuse, explain, and pretend. This space wasn't always safe either, needing as I do to love, learn, live, feel, know and forget.

Recently, I viewed a fine film which inspired for me another way of thinking about abuse victims who survive by the practice of vacating or absenting (metaphorically) the experience of abuse. In the film *To a Safer Place* (1987) Shirley Turcott talks with members of her family about her life as a survivor of childhood incest. Turcott discusses how she learned as a child to cope with abuse. She describes escaping, in her imagination, to the safety of the walls of the room in which she was abused. This enabled her to survive her father's abuse. I noted that her amazing survival technique was labelled *psychotic*. Fortunately Shirley was able to reject the negative connotations of this label, and in the film she talks about learning to view vacating as a critical and creative practice.

In a manner similar to Shirley, I used my imagination to escape the violence of my memories. To aid my survival, I learned to create comforting stories and memories of place, of woods, of crunchy leaves, of water, of salt air, and of magical libraries. These memories, like the places themselves, continue to remind me, to take me, to a place which has not known abuse. Thus, my escape into the *natural* allowed me to imagine that I was *normal*. In retrospect, I find it tragic that my need to be normal was *naturalized* through silence and repression. In this way, I did not know as a child that I had the right to say NO to abuse, although as an adult I would learn this right.

My experience of writing about abuse is significantly different than talking about it. As a victim of abuse I learned to distrust speech. Spoken words were unsafe because they represented my fear of speaking and the knowledge that I was living a lie. By contrast, I could hide among written words and pretend I was safe. In writing the words **I was sexually abused as a child**, I began to shift their importance by making conscious the abuse. When afraid, I still vacate my body (although this is less and less necessary). More in my body, I am learning to define and name the limits and boundaries of my own authority.

Like many women, I find it difficult to know my own authority. I have discovered, moreover, that many women learn to vacate their bodies for reasons other than sexual abuse. This other kind of vacating is well described in the work of Smith:

> We did not know how to view the world from where women are or were. We did not realize at first that our history was, in fact, not ours; that our sociology was not ours. We did not realize what was not there and was there. Becoming a feminist means taking these matters up deliberately as a course of action, since the very forms of our oppression means a deliberate remaking of our-

selves, our relations with others and our intellectual and cultural modes (1981:2)

Women are collectively negated by a history shaped and formed by male experience. From this perspective it is difficult, as Smith points out, for women to know the authority of their own voices. Smith ascertains that this way of organizing space is powerful and political in its systematic effacement of women's experience. Until women can reclaim and know authority, men will continue to abuse and victimize us and we will continue to please and follow men. Our society is organized to make it so (McMahon, 1986; Lewis, 1988).

My experiences of abuse and incest are not unique, only uniquely mine. In telling my story, I have constructed but one version of how my learning is connected to abuse. Unable to capture the nuances of this experience or the differing layers of analyses I use to know this abuse, I worry that I have created a ghostly figure who will disappear in the gaps and cracks of my writing. In Chapter 1, I have attempted to identify some of the values, aims and assumptions which underlie and motivate my work. In particular, implicit in my story is the assumption that I can examine the construction of my identity in order to get inside the less obvious fabric of ideologies which shape "the history my body has lived" (Rockhill, 1987:2), by the (re)construction of my social history through autobiographical narration.

In this chapter I suggest that autobiographical reflection and analysis is an effective way to begin breaking the social taboos which produce and reproduce such dichotomies as private and public. In making transparent, through story-telling, the divisions of socially constructed dualities, I think it is possible to better understand how our collective and individual identities are culturally produced. Importantly, through memory-work and the re-construction of our everyday experience, we can begin to challenge the worth of such separations, and thus disrupt those academic canons which dismiss experience as a basis for knowledge. In refusing to regard ourselves as victims, and through attempts to understand instead that "we have participated actively in the formation of our own past experience, then the usual mode of social-scientific research in which individuals figure exclusively as objects of the process of research, has to be abandoned" (Haug et al., 1987:35). This kind of knowing constitutes what I now understand as *critical consciousness*.

In my use of this term, I do not imply a right or final state of consciousness (Rockhill, 1987:47) but rather designation of a way of knowing which can be learned: a way which enables us to know ourselves as producers and users of knowledge within the very fabric of being, and to know ourselves as creators and dismantlers of ideologies (Williamson, 1981/82). In the following pages I will explore my assumption that this way of knowing can be learned within the context of schooling practices. I suggest this guardedly, for I also know that current schooling practices are generally not compatible with liberation for either women or men.

Love and Solidarity.

I think it is important to note that this story was not produced in one writing but rather, it is a story which emerged in a series of writings. Each writing produced yet another version, another story.

chapter two

A: Crises and Contradictions: Re-Viewing Ideology

One studies stories not because they are true or even because they are false, but for the same reason that people tell and listen to them, in order to learn about the terms on which others make sense of their lives: what they take into account and what they do not; what they consider worth contemplating and what they do not; what they are and are not willing to raise and discuss as problematic and unresolved in life (Brodkey, 1987:47).

I see us all sitting around naked, shivering, in a huge circle, looking up as the sky turns black and the stars flare out and somebody starts to tell a story, claims to see a pattern in the stars. And then someone else tells a story about the eye of the hurricane, the eye of the tiger. And the stories, the images, become the truth and we will kill each other rather than change one word of the story (French, 1977:386).

Knowing is the task of Subjects, not of objects. It is as a subject, and only as such, that a man or woman can really know (Freire, 1973:101).

*Chapter 1 is a narration, reflection and analysis of aspects of my social history. I suggested in Chapter 1 that writing is a powerful means for analyzing and shifting the effects of the various kinds of abuse which have shaped my understanding of self and hence my ability to engage in, or not engage in, certain social practices. My aim is to become conscious of the effects of abuse so that I can make real choices. In doing this work I am discovering that writing is an effective means of shifting outward the effects of an **internalized, naturalized** abuse. In the process of writing out these abuses I am rejecting the effects of **oppressors** whose authority I have internalized and whose power has silenced me in particular ways, making it difficult to choose from a place of self-authority. In this way I am beginning to reclaim my authority as a knower (Freire, 1970:33).*

*My aim in Chapter 2 is to introduce and begin to problematize some of the ways in which a series of events, practices and crises lead me to think about knowledge as socially constructed, and how this change enables me to theorize differently the relationship of sexual abuse to schooling practices. In narrating these events and crises my intent is to open up for discussion how coming to terms with sexual abuse enabled me to begin to really know, in terms described by Williamson, that much of what I once took for granted, or thought was natural, is socially constructed (1981:85). Specifically, I examine how my internalization and naturalization of abuse worked to keep me from acknowledgement of those abuses, thus allowing their effects to organize me according to an **illusion:** that my brother (male authority) had the **right** to abuse me. My silences affirmed this right. My intent in Chapter 2 is to examine some of the events and crises which propelled me toward analysis of my social history, my silences, and the relationship of my abuse to how I learn. While I do not assume my experiences to be universal, I do assume that analysis of stories such as mine might contradict many of the basic premises of critical educational theories.*

The illusion that male authority was natural and right did not, of course, work at all levels of my being. I asserted many of my social needs while continuing to grow and change. Nonetheless, my development and growth was circumscribed by an inability to name my oppression in a society organized to teach survivors silence. Not able to speak my abuse, I couldn't really know myself as a creator of my own knowledge. Thus I could not recognize knowledge as socially constructed except in a very limited way. My body worked to deny the information which my mind accepted. This was because I always assumed that the authority of the other (my oppressor) was more powerful than was my own authority. My body informed me so. In situations where I was expected to relate to authority figures, I (internally) tended to accept the authority of the other. Therefore, it was difficult for me to assume my own authority though at yet another level I consistently rebelled against outside authority. A simple example of this push/pull behaviour was forcing myself to speak in public (in front of other people) despite my overwhelming fear.

Dear Lily, Andrew and Virginia:

What, then, are some of the crises which lead me to write a thesis about feminist pedagogy from my perspective as a survivor of incest? What are the crises which enable me to *really* understand what it means to say that knowledge is socially organized and produced? How could I talk about the social construction of knowledge (the assumption that we are all creators and producers of knowledge), while reproducing social practices which contradict that assumption? Why did I not perceive this to be a contradiction? What crises enabled me to understand ideology as something which I, too, practice? Only recently am I able to ask these questions.

I think these questions are important. They are particularly important for educators wanting to understand gender oppression, knowledge as socially constructed, and how to teach themselves and others to critically examine all social practices. Like Williamson (1981/82), I am working to develop a critical pedagogy which will explicate the ideological practices shaping my own social practices as an educator. My assumption is that I can learn to help myself and my students to examine the practices organizing our experiences. This kind of approach to teaching can not, I suggest, be understood apart from an analysis of relations of power, subjectivity, gender, class and race (Weller, 1988; Livingstone, 1987). This approach does not, of course, begin from the assumption that there is one right way of *seeing* but rather, in keeping with Williamson, it begins from the assumption that "students learn best to 'see' the 'invisible', ideology, when it becomes in their own interest to — when they are actually caught in a contradiction . . . " (1981/82:85).

A series of contradictions, problems and crises enabled me — over a period of time — to question much of what I had previously taken for granted. This is, of course, an ongoing process. I do not imply that we ever reach a stage in our social relations where contradictions and crises do not exist, nor do we reach some final and perfect state of knowing, despite a continuing wish for harmony and contentment. With respect to my own crises, however, and the questions evoked, I am interested in understanding how I came to know in an intellectual way, which denied the validity of my bodily reactions. To clarify what I mean here I share with you my reactions to a particular crisis. I use this story because it demonstrates well my reactions to authority figures as a survivor of abuse and how I both learned and relearned abuse.

For a variety of reasons, I chose to complete my MA over a three-year period in a male-organized anthropology department. At times I felt uneasy with a professor who appeared uncomfortable with women students. Initially, I did not identify his behaviour as harassment. It was later, during my thesis defense that I most acutely experienced his power to harass. Chosen by my advisor to chair the defense, he was expected neither to ask questions nor offer opinions. He ignored this mandate and engaged in a twenty-minute tirade. He expressed a concern that my work was not objective. In his opinion, the topic of battered women could not constitute serious academic research. In words, tone and body language, he expressed and experienced his personal rage. I struggled hard to make sense of his academic criticism while responding to the questions of other attending persons.

In the aftermath of his tirade, he disturbed the defense in other equally objectionable ways. For example, he and another professor passed notes to one another. This disruption was readily apparent, yet no one stopped him, myself included. The extent of his rage and antagonism was made most apparent to me when, following the defense, he returned to me his copy of my thesis. Inside was the note which had been passed back and forth. In part, this note reads,

> Marilyn (his wife) asked me this morning if Anne-Louise would wear a low cut dress (to the defense). I said, "no, she will probably bring her Bull Dikes (sic) with her" (1982).

Presumably he thought I was in need of protection. This protection, he assumed further, would be in the form of a low-cut dress and the company of lesbians. This kind of subjective bias is dangerous, especially in a scholar who has the power and authority to pronounce on what is and is not objective.

At that time, I was unable to recognize his words as an attack on me or on the women with whom I worked. Instead, I was devastated by his power to conclude and proclaim that I was an unworthy scholar: I internalized his opinion that I was unable to produce an objective study. This made it difficult for me to believe that I did not deserve his abuse. At another level, I knew better. The less conscious part of my reaction dominated until I was able to critique his abuse at a much later time. In the interim, I struggled with his charge of non-objectivity.

Feeling inadequate and unable to confront the power of a professor who, for unstated reasons, felt free to express his subjective hatred, I produced, along with the thesis, an ulcer. This was not unlike my response as a young girl, powerless in my fear of confronting my brother's abuse. While it is clear now that *telling* might have freed me from years of silence, fear and pain, nothing in my experience then allowed me to consider this a real possibility. Similarly, I was unable to identify the actions of this professor as abusive. Battered women and victims of rape often describe similar feelings and reactions. Fear, helplessness, and internalized rage are common responses.

How abuse works to disrupt one's relationship to authority, particularly self-authority, is not difficult to understand once one accepts that the first instance of abuse makes it difficult thereafter for survivors to reclaim their authority. Prerequisite to this understanding, however, is an analysis of male violence against women. This critique remains an intellectual exercise unless survivors are able to unlearn trauma experienced at a pre-cognitive stage, or in other words, to feel the critique. This is because abuse is learned as a body memory. It is therefore difficult to unlearn at the level of cognition only. A number of abuse survivors have spoken to me about the need for body therapy as a means of releasing learned trauma. This kind of therapy might include dance or exercise and seems to be most helpful when used in conjunction with other forms of analysis as, for example, that which can occur in self-help groups.

The crisis I've just described remained internalized for many years. Within months of the event, however, I received a call from the dean of graduate studies. Her intent was to gather together several women students who felt they had been harassed by the professor in question. This action was precipitated by the work of a particular student who had decided to take action against him. At the time, I had begun my PhD work at a university quite some distance from the one in which this event had occurred. I was almost afraid to tell my story to the dean. I wasn't sure, until I sat in her office and felt the pain, that I had a story to tell. At one level I knew the behaviour of this professor was abusive. At another level I did not think I was worthy of better treatment. Significantly, I felt most concerned about his responses to my work: I worried about my ability to do objective research. Unable to critique his perspective, I remained a victim of his abuse. And so it was that my rage became internalized and focused on the search for a *better* method of doing research. In Chapter 3 I will return to this story.

B: Re-confronting the Limits of Social Knowledge: (my own, in particular)

> I would like to suggest another way to go further towards a new economy of power relations . . . It consists of taking the forms of resistance against different forms of power as a starting point (Foucault in Dreyfus, 1982: 210-211).

> The idea of ideology as something we all participate in, underlies the first possibility of critical thought, because it shows that no ideas are given or absolute. Without the notion of cultural relativism, truly questioning thought is impossible, because our own premises are never questioned. The more I have taught in further education, the more I think it hardly matters, in a way, what you teach, as long as it leads to this questioning, which itself is a prerequisite for social change (Williamson, 1981/82:83).

Continuing my academic studies at another university did not help me find a better method of doing research. I did, however, begin to analyze how relations of power worked to silence me and others in the classroom. This awareness developed in a class of equal numbers of women and men. As a participant, I began to confront seriously the problem of why and how male students are able to dominate class discussions. I was curious to know how it was that women were doing the readings for the course and yet were often silent during discussion (see the work of Lewis and Simon, 1986). This silence was particularly disturbing as I realized that class discussions were being dominated by male students whose comments did not appear related to the material being examined. That we were quiet was frustrating to me. I knew we had done the readings. My initial response to my own silence was fear that I had not read the material *correctly*. I assumed, moreover, that if I had read it *correctly* my silence would end. In other words, if I and the other women in the class could better comprehend the material, the men in the class would not dominate the discussions. I believed that improved methods and greater knowledge would solve the problem of women's silence in the classroom. I didn't know then about gender inequality at other than the intuitive level.

Driven by the need to find a better methodology for my work and by a desire to break the silences controlling many of the women in the classes

I attended, I decided to change my program of study. Mid-stream I moved to a faculty of education largely populated by feminist scholars. Here I felt affirmed both as a learner and as a woman. Interestingly, however, I remained unable to speak in this new environment for a number of months. In part, my speechlessness was due to awe, not fear. I was overwhelmed by excitement and joy in classrooms where women and a few men were sharing ideas, personal stories, responses to materials, and power. I do not want to suggest that this kind of sharing was easy. It was not. Rather, learning occurred as students struggled with materials and with relations of power. In this context I began to reclaim aspects of the power lost to me through abuse.

Despite my immersion in feminist perspectives, I remained unable to see a connection between the abuses I had experienced and my desire to discover a *true*, objective method of research. I continued to believe in a more accurate way of working with the stories of battered women. In reading the work of Rockhill, I began to consider the limitations of intellectual endeavours which did not allow for emotional responses. More specifically, I began to consider how a non-emotional academic perspective might prevent me from understanding oppression (1986:13).

It was in this state of contemplation that I confronted for the first time ever the abuse I had been subjected to as a child. It is not surprising that this confrontation occurred in the context of story-telling. Two stories changed the direction of my life. One was Rockhill's tale of sexual abuse and the other was McIntyre's tale of abuse in the academy. In hearing these two stories, I was thrown into a major crisis. It was, however, a crisis of a different sort. This time I felt hope as well as fear.

In the wake of this crisis, I could neither sleep nor work. I struggled with the implications of the stories. Questions exploded inside of me. How could I make sense of scholars and authority figures willing to speak openly about their respective, differing abuses? Moreover, how could I make sense of their insistence that it was theoretically significant to speak about these kinds of abuses? What about my own abuse? It was one thing to hear about the abuse of others, but could I talk about my own? These questions haunted me. I knew I was closer to confronting the splits which had organized so many years of my life. How could I take seriously my abuses and what would it mean to speak of them in an academic context? How could I make sense of something of which, like Rockhill (1987), I was fearful to speak:

> We don't let ourselves know in part because we are terrified to see, and then to name and live by what we see. Feminism carried with it the terror of separation,

aloneness, isolation — for the enemy that it names is man — and even if we know that he is also a victim of domination through the prescriptive mandates of masculinity — he still lives out his violence through us, through our bodies, through his control over us in every aspect of our lives (14)?

C: Breaking the Cycle/Circle

I first, really learnt, that my ideas were not my **own** and that our social reality is ideological, not through media studies but a sociology course in my first year at university. Reading a particular book, at a time of uncertainty in a new environment, changed my perception of everything ever since (Williamson, 1981/82:85).

The Key point . . . is that our minds and bodies are the primary sites of our oppression and that the very formation of our subjectivities is political (Rockhill, 1987).

In the midst of the crisis I have just described, I read a book which provoked in me a multitude of reactions and responses and subsequently altered my view of the world. This book was instrumental in my decision to change the focus of my research from battered women to a reconstruction of how I am shaped by abuse. Excited and frustrated by *Women's Ways of Knowing: Development of Self, Voice, and Mind* (Belenky et al., 1986) I read and reread the book. I argue elsewhere that it is problematic because of the authors' tendency to overlay very important data with a new version of an old theoretical perspective (Brookes, 1988). Documenting in depth the relationship of sexual abuse to women's learning and development, I think the book fails to address seriously the implications of their findings.

Specifically, the book draws from the work of Perry (1970). Perry's work is a study of developmental theory derived from his analysis of male students attending Harvard University. This study is still considered by educators and researchers to be a definitive work. Perry's theories are still used as a guide for educators, Belenky et al. included. In this early work, Perry assumes that it is not problematic to use this research to indiscriminately chart the epistemological development of both female and male students, despite the fact that his work originates in male experience.

Perry assumes that students move in a linear way, from a basic dualism where the world is viewed in terms of black/white, right/ wrong, through to increasingly advanced stages. In the last stage one is presumed to know that all knowledge is relative and socially constructed. Perry assumes further "that dualists are rare at Harvard" (1970:63).

Critical of his assumption that students learn in a linear manner, Belenky et al. do argue that Perry's development scheme cannot be readily applied to the experience of women (9), noting that "women's thinking did not fit so neatly into his categories" (14), particularly women's experiences of male authority (23-34). Their work, however, does build on Perry's scheme when they argue that women's learning can be grouped into "five major epistemological categories" (15). Also problematic, I think, is their assumption that women learn differently than men, and therefore require a woman-centered education (214-229).

The assumption that women learn in intrinsically different ways than men is troublesome for me when it is used to argue, as they do, that women require only a new kind of education based on their difference. At one level, I do not agree with this theoretical position. Specifically, I fear that this kind of pedagogy would forever isolate women in an academic context which is already highly stratified. I do not wish to imply here that women students do not benefit greatly from a safe and supportive learning environment. My experience suggests otherwise. Women's studies programs demonstrate well the need for safe learning environments.

What concerns me, however, is that Belenky et al. do not address the need for safety as a political problem. Rather, they locate the problem in differences between women and men. I am not certain that structural changes for women only will ultimately benefit women. What is needed is an educational system committed to the development of classrooms in which women and men can analyze how their abilities to access power differ, and see relations of power as socially constructed. Without this kind of analysis, men will continue to use and abuse power and women will continue to be ruled by male abuse. Presupposed here, of course, is that critical educational theories and practices will benefit both women and men. Also presupposed is that men will choose to do this work. To make this choice demands, of course, that men move beyond the limitations of Perry's work: I suggest that learners cannot know that knowledge is constructed and at the same time ignore how relations of power differently organize gender, race and class, unless, of course, the learner is immoral.

Love and Solidarity.

My aim in Chapter 2 was to introduce and discuss a series of crises which compelled me to critique the various ways in which abuse shaped my learning experiences. Specifically, my aim was to critique the idea that learning can be definitively categorized and catalogued. Through narration and analysis, my intent was to illustrate the great complexity of learning and development.

While I agree with Perry and Belenky et al. that students can move from dualism to the relativist perspective that all knowledge is socially constructed, I argue that learning does not occur as they suggest, in a hierarchical, stage-like manner, but rather it can occur over and over again in the context of everyday practices. These practices can produce contradictions which subjects can recognize and address in relation to others. I began my analysis from the assumption that students and teachers can be taught to critique the socially-produced political perspectives which shape and organize educational practices. Such critiques can result in crises for those who take up this kind of work.

chapter three

A: Perspectives and Approaches

Autobiography, like teaching, combines two perspectives, one that is a distanced view—rational, reflective, analytic and one that is close to its subject matter—immediate, filled with energy and intention (Grumet, 1981:211).

How do I set about writing the story of an event from my early childhood? My aim is to gain from past feelings and connections some knowledge of the way we work ourselves into the social world. One of the difficulties is that past feelings and thoughts may be distorted by present-day value-judgements; . . . I attempt then to develop a method which can be applied generally to such memories. For the scene I want to reproduce, I look for a key image . . . . (Haug et al., 1987:71).

The stories which I constructed and began to analyze in Chapters 1 and 2 are key to the organization of this book. I wrote the stories to better understand how I am affected by my experiences of abuse, as well as to examine my assumption that autobiographical reflection is a legitimate way of doing academic research. My aim in Chapter 3 is to introduce readers to the work of Grumet (1981) and Haug et al. (1987). These authors interest me because their work supports my theoretical assumption that autobiographical writing is a valid methodological approach. From a focus on their perspectives, my aim is to examine how to use autobiography to write beyond the abuses which shape and inform me. Lastly, from a focus on how I presently use the term feminist pedagogy, I will consider briefly the use of autobiography in my current teaching practices.

Dear Lily, Andrew and Virginia:

I am writing this morning to discuss with you how the work of Grumet (1981) and Haug et al. (1987) is key to the way I am writing my thesis. I will speak first about my reading of Grumet because it was through her work that I began to understand autobiography as an important way of *doing* academic work. No less important to me, however, is my reading of Haug et al.

Following my decision to write about my experiences of abuse, I discovered Grumet's work on autobiography. Quite frankly, I was looking for theoretical justification for my decision to write autobiographically. I wanted a scholar to demonstrate that autobiography was a legitimate way of doing academic research. I first found this support in an essay written by Grumet entitled *Autobiography and Reconceptualization* (1981) in which she theorizes her use of autobiography as a teaching and research tool. Key to this essay is Grumet's assumption that "This work is pursued in the aspiration that it will enable the student to become the active interpreter of his (sic) past as well as heighten his capacity to be the active agent of his own interests in a present that he shares with his community" (14).

I was delighted to read Grumet's essay because, as an abuse survivor, I wanted to reconceptualize the social practices which had taught me to "not know" abuse. Pragmatically, I felt that Grumet's essay provided a means of examining the ongoing effects of abuse in my life. As I began the long process of writing, I understood better the immense difficulties in reconceptualizing those stories which shape my past and present.

To begin the reconceptualization process, Grumet suggests that students write an "essay that provides at least three narratives of events in their lives that they would call educational experiences. The stories need not concern schooling, but they may" (12). In this first phase Grumet urges students to carefully construct their stories, with considerable attention to detail and description. It is this, she suggests, which will enable them to begin the second phase of reclaiming and reconceptualizing their stories (12).

In the second phase students analyze their stories. The intent is to examine carefully the apparent and not so apparent interests, biases, and assumptions used to organize the stories. This process may or may not involve a teacher. As teacher, however, she responds to student writing for the explicit purpose of helping "the writer to ascertain what is missing in the text as well as to recognize patterns and themes that often surface in each of the apparently disparate narratives" (14). With respect to her teacher responses Grumet is wise, I think, to suggest that she intends to help the writer maintain "possession and authority over his (sic) prose." She notes, in fact, that the student "need not respond to any questions which call him (sic) into territory he'd (sic) rather not tread" (14).

The work of Haug et al. (1987), like that of Grumet (1981), is unusual in its attempt to theorize autobiography as a method of reconceptualization. However, unlike Grumet, Haug and others use themselves as the objects of their own research (p. 50). Their aim is to "study the way in which human beings construct themselves into the world" (52). Key to their analysis is a theoretical explanation of their use of stories as a kind of memory work to examine the "points of disjuncture between our stories of childhood and the way of life we mark out for ourselves today" (51). In their opinions, to understand these disjunctures is to begin the process of un-learning old and re-learning new patterns of socialization (65). They assume that "Writing and analyzing stories is amongst other things a way of gaining self-confidence," (65) and simultaneously, a "basis of questioning our own ideological socialization" (50).

It is not, however, just any kind of writing which Haug et al. employ as a means of questioning their own patterns of socialization. It is, in fact, a collective writing process which involves "collective discussions . . ." (49). The reason for this collective writing and discussion is to "reach a point at which we no longer see ourselves through the eyes of others" (39). In this manner, writing is both a "weapon of defense" and a tool of creativity (39), they suggest. Hence, writing is a means of creating and destroying the power of a dominant culture (38). They suggest further that autobiographical writing is a way of working "our way through and into ideology" (44). For the purpose of examining "this process and events in the past in new and more or less unprejudiced ways" (47). In their opinions, training for this process involves teaching the eye to see the values and assumptions which shape social practices. In this way writing is a reflective way of de-naturalizing "ourselves and our actions, thoughts and feelings" (58).

I am profoundly touched by the ideas expressed in the work of Haug et al. At every level, their ideas support my desire to write an autobiographical thesis. At this time, however, I cannot imagine how I might make this a (consciously) collective, rather than solitary, endeavour. Caught in the demand of singular thesis production, I draw more from Grumet's (1981) approach and less from the approach devised by Haug et al. (1987).

When writing and analyzing the stories in my text, I began, as suggested by Grumet, by allowing myself to free-associate and reflect on the experiences which make up these stories (Grumet, 1981:12). Through the process of writing and thinking reflexively about these stories, I began to reconceptualize the experiences. Through attention to detail, I attempt, as Grumet suggests, to reclaim aspects of the past and present not readily apparent to me. From this process of reclamation, I can sometimes better understand my silences and the practices which produce my silence.

Much of this reclamation, I am discovering, is dependent upon the quality of questions which supervisors ask in reading my work. It is here that I best understand my work as a collective endeavour, though not the kind described by Haug and others. Equally important, I think, is my desire to learn how to ask good questions of my own writing. In reading Grumet's work, I do not think she theorizes sufficiently the relationship of good questions to the production of reflexive writing. This relationship is better addressed by Haug et al.

In the second phase of my reclaiming project, I attempt to analyze my stories for the explicit purpose of discovering "interests and biases we rarely see because they are threaded through the thick fabric of our daily lives" (Grumet, 1981:13). It is in this second phase of reconceptualizing that I begin to see differently some of the ways in which I am organized by dominant ideologies. And it is in this second phase, writes Grumet, that I begin to see more consciously "where I am and where I am going" (13). Key to seeing this is a willingness and ability to bring myself close to my writings in both feeling and analytical ways. Through this closeness, I can see differently how oppression works. I begin to see the difficulties of writing as an abuse survivor and as a woman researcher who has been taught to ghost write from a male perspective (Campbell, 1987:2).

In my opinion, neither Grumet nor Haug et al. theorize sufficiently the questions of what constitutes collective writing or whether individuals (alone) can work reflexively with their own writings, which of course we do. Implied is the assumption that autobiography is a dialogue between teacher and student: the student writes and the teacher responds to the writing. A dialogue occurs to the extent that students can choose how to respond to the teacher's comments. This kind of dialogue differs, however, from that described by Haug et al. in whose text there are no teachers, only individuals collectively writing and sharing their stories. By contrast, Grumet does not theorize her own stories, as do the writers in the group described by Haug et al. Rather, she responds to the work of students. Thus, the assumptions which organize her responses are not necessarily examined by others. For this reason it is possible to imagine power imbalances occurring between student and teacher. Similarly, I recognize the possibility that such an imbalance might occur between committee members and myself in the production of my thesis. The group process described by Haug et al. could potentially check these kinds of inequities.

Following Grumet, I think it is important for teachers who work with autobiographical material to ensure that writers retain their own authority. In other words, while readers are always *entitled* to responses based on their experience, it is important to keep in mind that dialogue and analysis arise out of discussion, sharing and questioning. They do not come from the assertions of authorities who impose analysis rather than ask of the other what she or he means by a particular writing. Without this kind of dialogue subjects stand to be dehumanized by an autobiographical approach to research which, in theory, is designed to liberate writers from oppressive social practice.

Love and Solidarity.

B: Feminist Pedagogy In/Formation

> The basic problem is not how to get women's studies accepted in departments of sociology . . . but how it is possible, and what it means, to be a feminist sociologist and practice an activity which one believes can accurately be called feminist sociology (Oakley, 1986:205).

Dear Lily, Andrew and Virginia:

The intent of my most recent letter to you was to indicate how I am using the autobiographical research methods of Grumet (1981) and Haug et al. (1987). In today's letter I want to discuss the title of my thesis, Feminist Pedagogy: a Subject In/Formation, and why I assume I am writing about feminist pedagogy. Supported by feminist scholars, I first began to know, from a critical perspective, that I was abused. This knowing, however, is not static. Rather, it shifts and changes, as does the subject matter.

What then do I mean when I use the title Feminist Pedagogy? If you recall, I began the Preamble with a quote from Weedon, who writes that "Feminism is a politics. It is a politics directed at changing existing power relations between women and men in society. These power relations structure all areas of life . . . They determine who does what and for whom, what we are and what we might become" (1927:1). I quote

Weedon because she defines so very well how I understand and experience feminism. I find her words as powerful. They allow me to imagine how I and others can move beyond abuse. They encourage me to examine, name, and expose relations of power which support abuse. They enable me to imagine feminist pedagogies which may alter the practices and politics of abuse.

What I have just described as feminism is not, however, some new kind of truth. Rather, feminism is a perspective from which to examine relations of power (see the work of Smith, 1987). To examine relations of power is, in my opinion, to examine how they differently organize sexualities, genders, races and classes. Because I start from the assumption that the focus of a feminist perspective is a critique of power and how people are differently organized by relations of power, I therefore insist that feminism is a political perspective(s) (I assume here that all perspectives are political) which must be taken up by women and men of all races and classes. Feminism is not a perspective for women only.

From my understanding of feminist perspectives, I view myself as both the subject of this text and the subject producing it. In naming myself as the subjective self producing this work, I theoretically shift from a truth perspective to one which I hope enables readers (and me) to see me as a producer and maker of knowledge. From this perspective, I am beginning to better understand the concept of knowledge as socially constructed. I can also better appreciate the importance of autobiography as method. In other words, until I understood myself as a producer of knowledge, I could not consciously or politically analyze, from a perspective of power, the male-constructedness of this society.

It is in this process of analyzing relations of power that feminists understand the theoretical importance of placing themselves at the centre of the research process. It is in the discovery that it is difficult to include women's experience in mainstream bodies of knowledge without changing how knowledge is produced that a feminist perspective emerges. Though critical and Marxist scholars long ago identified the knowledge problem in the research process, many are unable yet to theorize the importance of using gender as a point of departure. By contrast, my reading of feminist scholarship suggests that placing myself at the centre of the research process in a male-organized society is, in fact, to do critical feminist research.

The term 'critical' alone does not address adequately how women and men as real live acting gendered subjects actually experience oppression and power. I use the term feminist because it is predominantly feminist research which names and analyzes power and oppression from a focus on how subjects of either sex experience oppression and power in the context of sexuality, gender, race and class. In my opinion, a critical perspective is too far removed from acting subjects and how they understand themselves as producing knowledge. However, should men begin to work from a feminist perspective, to focus on the gender system woven through sexualities, races, and classes, it is theoretically possible that a new term will emerge to replace the term feminist. That is unless, of course, women and men agree to keep the term in honour of positive changes initiated by the work of feminism.

In my attempts to develop feminist pedagogies, much of what I do in the classroom involves re-visioning "the politics of truth" (Meese, 1986) for the purpose of seeing more clearly how knowledge is socially constructed. Specifically, I am trying to devise teaching practices which enable students to understand relations of power, and how social practices differently benefit women and men, races and classes. To do this, I draw extensively from the work of Smith (1987) who, in Oakley's terms, has begun to identify a practice which could most "accurately be called feminist sociology" (Oakley, 1986:205).

I have struggled for some time with the term 'feminist sociology'. Initially, I could not perceive the difference between feminist sociology and women's studies. However, as a result of my attempts to use a feminist perspective in a mixed-gender classroom, I am beginning to understand my assumptions about both feminist sociology and women's studies. I have discovered, for example, that it is possible for scholars in a women's studies program to work from a non-feminist perspective. It is also possible to work from a feminist perspective in a non-women's studies program. It is this work which I identify as feminist sociology. Thus, I am in agreement with Oakley's assumption that "The basic problem is not how to get women's studies accepted in departments of sociology . . . but how it is possible, and what it means, to be a feminist sociologist and practice an activity which one believes can accurately be called feminist sociology" (205).

I am interested in the theoretical differences between what it means to do feminist sociology and women's studies because I know that many of us who graduate from institutions in which we have been *allowed* to write from feminist perspectives will not have the luxury of teaching in a women's studies program. Instead, many of us will take up teaching, if we are fortunate enough to find positions, in universities where we will teach both female and male undergraduate students with little or no interest in feminist perspectives. In part, this lack of interest is based on misconceptions about what constitutes a feminist perspective. I'm discovering that once students are introduced to feminism as a means of understanding the social organization of power and knowledge, their interest is activated. This is so, I think, because they enjoy relating academic material to themselves.

It is important (at least for me) to understand how feminist perspectives might prove valuable to the learning experiences of both women and men. My research is helping me and could potentially help other educators to develop new pedagogical ways of working with a wide range of students in traditional academic programs. My aim is both political and partial. I begin from the assumption that my work is but a part of a much larger body of feminist scholarship. I do not assume that feminist pedagogies will change students but I do assume that the work which I and others do from these perspectives is both necessary and important. At the very least it is a perspective which attempts to create a space for possible transformations.

Specifically, I am to explore ways in which autobiography can be used in a classroom setting for the specific purpose of developing a critical consciousness, through taking up issues of sexuality, gender, race, class, and power in any academic context. This attempt to address explicitly notions of critical consciousness and gender is not apparent in much of the current work on educational practices. I will take up this assumption in the latter part of my letter. Just now, however, I want to share with you some of how my current teaching practices are informing the work of my thesis, and conversely, how these teaching practices are informed by a feminist perspective which begins from a consciously subject/ive analysis of relations of power.

Teaching undergraduate sociology students. Sometimes I feel more frustrated and exhausted than I have felt in my entire life. I am frustrated because, on one hand, I feel privileged to be working in an environment where I can experiment pedagogically, and on the other, I feel that my graduate studies did not adequately prepare me to do the work of teaching. Common to most graduate schools is the tendency to develop student research skills rather than teaching skills. It is difficult to implement creative and critical reading and writing skills when exhausted by the work of teaching, and in my case, lone-parenting. Positively, my teaching experience is enabling me to think more concretely about my research, in particular how schooling practices shape and inform teachers and students. Teaching, I'm discovering, is exciting work, especially as I struggle to work from feminist perspectives.

During the summer term at Memorial University, I taught two courses in the general studies program. One was a fourth-level course in gender relations and the other was a third-level course in social theory. In this latter class there was an even distribution of women and men. Most of the students in both classes, which I organized in similar ways using different materials, had not been introduced to feminist perspectives. Despite the size of the classes, I arranged them into large seminar groups. My aim was to use specific materials, in specific ways, for the purpose of problematizing—from a focus on relations of power—issues of sexuality, gender, race and, class.

To do this, I requested that students work closely with one so-called theoretical core text in conjunction with three complementary texts. All assignments were structured to lead the students through the course in a way which would accommodate my interest in analyzing relations of power, while providing a (safe) space in which they could ask questions of the text. They did this in writings based upon their own experiences, interests, and assumptions, all of which inform how they read the texts.

In the social theory seminar, for example, I selected a recently published text by Sydie called *Natural Women, Cultured Men: A Feminist Perspective on Sociological Theory* (1987) as the core text. Although the text critiques the work of Durkheim, Weber and Marx from a feminist perspective, I found that I had, at times, to supplement it with other readings. As we worked our respective ways through the text, each student was required to do a presentation based on her or his reading of one part. At the same time, students were required to read, in a particular order, three other books: *Life with Billy*, (Vallee, 1986) a biographical account of one woman's life with a violent partner; *In Search of April Raintree*, (Culleton, 1983), an autobiographical account of two Métis sisters, which includes a powerful discussion of rape and suicide; and Atwood's novel *The Handmaid's Tale* (1985) which is, among other things, a fictional, futuristic critique of modern society.

I structured the course into three sections, so that when we were taking up Durkheim's theory of suicide in our core text, for example, we were simultaneously taking up Culleton's more personal, discussion of suicide. When examining Jane Stafford's experience of living with a man who battered her, we were simultaneously engaged in reading the section in the core text which addresses Weber's notion of ideal types, patriarchy and power. In the last section, when we took up Marx and Engels, social class, and the "woman question", we read Atwood's novel.

In all three sections I helped students ask explicit questions of the material with respect to power, sex, gender, race, and class. In part I did this by paying close attention to what I had observed to be of interest to each student. Hence, I could relate specific ideas to specific interests. I encouraged students to write autobiographically. A careful reading of their varied writing exercises enabled me to ask questions which were individually meaningful. In making this process clear to students, I was able to teach them how to then question their own writings. I also worked to clarify my assumptions about my readings of texts, stating always that these were *my* assumptions. Through a conscious explanation of this process, I think I also helped students identify and name the assumptions which organized their work, and ultimately, mine and others.

In this class, I discovered that the best way to teach students how to critique assumptions and how to ask questions is to require of them an abundance of reading, to which they must respond both in writing and in discussion. Each student was required to critique all the complementary texts. Instruction about what I expected in a critique, as opposed to a book review, was given early in the course.

Many students, I discovered, did not recognize the difference between a critique and being critical. Instructions for critiques, by which I mean understanding how a text is organized to present a particular perspective, were repeated in a variety of ways throughout the course. When critiquing the complementary accounts, I requested that students focus on (preferably) questions of interest which had arisen in their readings of the accounts. I encouraged them to look in their readings for the assumptions upon which writers developed theories, both in fictional and non-fictional forms. In my responses to students' works, I often queried their assumptions about the readings. My intent was to help them better see how theory is developed from the practices of everyday lives. Ultimately, I encouraged them to see themselves, and me as a teacher, as theory makers. They in turn queried me about my assumptions and questions concerning their work.

When writing critiques, students were expected to address simultaneously an aspect of the core text and a major idea or theme in the complementary text. Thus, while taking up Culleton's account of suicide, students were also required to address whether Durkheim's theory of suicide was in any way helpful to their understanding of it. My intent in bringing together these two texts was to give more concrete examples of theory than are usually encountered in theoretical accounts (even feminist ones). This way of using theory and fiction, I discovered, helps to alleviate students' fear of theory.

At all times I encouraged students to use their critiques as opportunities to write about their own experiences, if they so chose. I also encouraged them to use the experiences of others, as expressed in the novels, to understand specific theories or concepts. In practice, the work of the critiques was a form of autobiography whether or not students took up their own experiences, insofar as students worked hard to identify their own assumptions about ideology.

My responses to student writings were usually typed, two or three pages in length, and often in letter form. As learned from my reading of

Grumet (1981), I attempted to ask questions which might allow them to see and analyze themes and patterns in their own work. Often, I asked a question which I thought might lead to another question for the next critique. If their critiques were explicitly homophobic, sexist, or racist in style or content, I suggested, in writing, that I thought this was the case and how they might consider or alter these oppressive practices.

Because I took the work of novels seriously as an alternative means of producing theory, students learned to feel more relaxed in the classroom, to talk about personal experience. Thus students could begin to theorize from a more familiar place. As I expected, they readily related to the biographical and fictional accounts. Discussions of these accounts were emotional and intense, with students willing to compare their own experiences with the characters in the texts. I, too, shared my own experiences in the context of certain issues arising in our discussions.

In time, students easily identified the aims and assumptions of both kinds of accounts, theory and fiction/autobiography. Because they felt they had something useful to contribute to class discussions based on their ability to relate to so-called non-theoretical accounts, I found students more willing and able to tackle the theories of Weber, Durkheim and Marx. In so doing, they learned well how to critique the implicit and explicit assumptions of these writers, and hence to see them as not all that different from writers of autobiography and fiction. Excitingly, students began to see how various authors construct theory and, in seeing this, seemed more willing to construct their own assumptions and theories based on their own social practices.

Upon completion of the course a significant number of students told me they had had major shifts in their learning and thinking as a result of taking up the above-mentioned works in this (structured) manner. In bringing theory and practice together through reading, writing and simultaneous analysis of two different kinds of texts/readings, I believe some students discovered in themselves new strengths and new ways of seeing how we, and others, organize society.

Through intense discussions of power, sexuality, gender, race, and class in the context of readings not necessarily feminist in perspective or content (though taken up from my perspective of relations of power organized in particular ways), I discovered that students wrote critiques which were often autobiographical in content. In other words, they learned not to write in the detached manner of the review style, instead constructing in-depth critiques of the material from their subjective perspectives. Quite often, students used personal experiences as a means of resisting, and accommodating, their readings of a given text. As a result, I was able to work quite differently with their written texts because many of their aims and assumptions were readily apparent. In other words, I was able to address (through questioning their work) issues of power, sexuality, gender, race and class in their own texts and thus create a space in which they could potentially experience the merging of practice and theory. My aim was to show students, through example, how to question the assumptions which organize their texts, written or otherwise. I begin from the assumption that this is for me, and perhaps for all students, a life-long work.

In my other courses that fall I repeated this general pattern using different texts (mostly because I like reading and using new texts) to construct different kinds of questions, about different concerns. The format was basically the same. Whatever the text, I attempted to teach students how to critique, relations of power.

Based on my work with students who have not been directly exposed to feminist perspectives, I am discovering that it is useful to work with texts which produce emotional responses. Autobiographical fictions and biographies, for example, work well to inspire discussion. Generally, I choose books which I imagine will be of interest to my students as individuals living in a particular country, province, or community.

Fiction is a useful tool to help students consider the implicit and explicit assumptions which organize all works, including the assumptions I use to organize the course and those which they use to construct their works. My choices of texts, however, are biased and do not always reflect the interests of the students; rather, they reflect my assumptions about what students are interested in or learn from. When texts do not reflect their interests, it is readily apparent. When this occurs, I use the experience to talk about why I chose a particular text, and in turn, why they do not like it. I also ask students to talk about books which are of interest to them. In working in this manner my intent is to begin developing ways to break down some socially constructed dichotomies now acting as major *truths*. These are but a few of the practices which inform my attempts to teach from feminist perspectives.

In talking about my teaching experiences from a perspective which I identify as feminist, I do not wish to imply that there is only one way to teach from a feminist perspective. Nor do I wish to imply that there was no resistance to my pedagogical approach. There was. (For the most part resistance was met and dealt with as it arose. Often I learned from these experiences, as did the students.) Rather, my aim in this letter is to share some of the teaching methods I have developed based on my subjective experience as a woman who is an abuse survivor, but who is also informed and shaped by graduate school practices which teach me to critique the effects of relations of power from my subjective experience.

Theoretically, I aim in both my thesis and my pedagogical approaches to create new ways to unite theory and practice, while splitting apart socially produced dichotomies such as private and public, theory and practice, and objective and subjective. Like other educators who work to reduce socially constructed oppression, my intent is to create new and safer spaces in which to bring together the private and the public. In attempting to create a place, in an academic setting, where students can talk about their own experiences using academic works, I am learning how we can begin to talk, albeit with resistance, about difficult issues such as rape, male violence, and incest. These are issues that at one time could not be spoken about in public and were certainly not considered serious academic subjects.

In breaking through these dichotomies, we begin to dismantle the underpinnings of the social structure which sustains power relations between women and men. This, in my opinion, is revolutionary work which can be done by both women and men, in the context of our everyday schooling practices. It is, difficult political work which has at its centre the assumption that knowledge is socially produced and organized to differently benefit men and women. Therefore, it is the work of teachers to create and devise pedagogies which teach learners how to transform those structures of authority which produce oppression.

C: Punctuating the Dominant Order

My father did what he did because it allows him to do what he does (Atwood, 1983:244).

A university education, in its methodology and values if not always in its subject matter, is an induction into masculine thought processes, a preparation for a male career pattern. Universities are hierarchical institutions ... As well as being a hierarchy built on exploitation, the university is a breeding ground for masculine values: of competitiveness, of status-seeking, of public accomplishment, of the supposed supremacy of so-called **objectivity and scientific neutrality** (Oakley, 1986:203).

In the latter part of this letter, I want to further develop some of my assumptions about academic research. In particular, I am concerned about the recent theoretical directions implied in the works of Chodorow (1978), Gilligan (1982), and Belenky et al. (1986). Specifically, I want to return briefly to Belenky et al., whose work draws extensively from that of Chodorow and Gilligan.

Common to these educators is the assumption that women learn and know differently than men. Belenky et al. make this assumption and set out to develop a model of education for women based on the implied superiority of women's ways. Lacking in their analysis is any attention to the ways in which learning and knowing are political practices. While there is much to be gained from reading this text about women's relation to authority and male violence, I primarily use it as a theoretical point of resistance, rupture, and departure.

In Chapter 2, I argue that Belenky et al. (1986) do not address adequately how women's way of knowing is a political activity. This lack is problematic, I think, in a research project designed to draw conclusions about *knowledge, authority, and the truth* (3) of women's ways of knowing and learning. The authors, dissatisfied with evaluative methods and learning strategies which do not accommodate what they term women's *preferred learning style* (5), a form of intuitive knowing, attempt to devise a theory about how women and men learn and know *differently*.

Building on the work of William Perry (15), Belenky et al. organize women's perspectives on learning, based on their research data, into five epistemological categories. These are: *silence, received knowledge, subjective knowledge, procedural knowledge,* and *constructed knowledge*. While the authors clearly state that these are not universal categories, that they are abstract and hence cannot capture the complexity of individual women's thought, and that men show evidence of similar categories (15), implied in their work, nonetheless, is the assumption that one stage builds upon the other in a linear and hierarchical manner. I find this problematic from a methodological perspective because it lends itself, as does Perry's research, to an analysis which depends upon fitting experience into defined categories rather than attempting to make sense of that which does not fit; in this case, how women's learning is affected by male abuse. Instead, Belenky et al. assert the relationship of abuse to women's learning and conclude that a new model of education must be devised *for women*. Lost is an analysis of how men abuse or of how women know this abuse in an educational context.

Methodologically, Belenky et al. do not begin their study from a named assumption about the relationship of male violence to women's educational experiences. What they discover from their interviews with women, however, is that it is **shockingly common** for women to speak about experiences of male abuse and incest in conversations about education. So common is it that midway through the study the authors systematically built this factor into their theoretical framework (58).

Moreover, from their work with women both inside and apart from the classroom, Belenky et al. conclude that "education and clinical service as traditionally defined do not serve the needs of women..." (4). When, for example, women were questioned about learning shifts in their ways of knowing, the authors found that knowledge shifts appear to have little to do with education as narrowly defined. For many women,

> Instead of opening the world up to them, the kind of education and educators they encountered as children and adolescents were alienating and irrelevant to their lives. To us, it appeared that it was only after some crisis of trust in male authority in their daily lives, coupled with some confirmatory experience that they, too, could know something for sure, that women ... could take steps to change their fate and "walk away from the past" (58).

Significantly, Belenky et al. discovered that sexual harassment, abuse and incest form a pervasive background story in the lives of the one hundred and thirty-five women surveyed. Of the college women interviewed, one in five described a history of childhood incest. Among those interviewed from social agencies, one in two was a victim of incest. Within the context of how women learn and know, therefore, male violence, as demonstrated in this sample, is not easily dismissed.

In telling my story, I suggest it is difficult for women who experience male abuse as adolescents to learn self-authority, in that abuse damages one's relationship to any authority figure. In part, I think this is true because the violence occurs during an extremely vulnerable learning time when it is not easily expressed as a problem. The trauma of these experiences informs the adolescent's education, resulting in a learned silence. This, of course, affects future learning. Only when victims of abuse are able to make conscious (and body learn) the abuse does it become possible to shift from an internalized male authority and imposed forms of silence (69). As the work of Belenky et al. demonstrates, male abuse impedes women's learning. This is not unconnected to the fact that women, through male abuse, are taught to doubt our achievements (60).

It is important, I think, to continually connect male abuse with the social practices which organize and condone it. Academic institutions and practices, as Oakley points out, are designed to produce and reproduce "masculine values" (1986:203), as well as the "supposed supremacy of so-called **objectivity** and **scientific neutrality**" (203). While Belenky et al. argue for a new model of education based on women's experience, they do not sufficiently address a) their own discovery that only a few women in their study, because of experiences in the home, are able to move beyond the "epistemological atmosphere depicted in their family histories" (155) — family being where women experience male abuse — and b) the gender-based constructions of academic practices producing dominant notions of objectivity and neutrality. Thus, while the study indicates that abuse *may* affect women's ways of learning and knowing, it does not examine *how* it does, or does not, affect women's knowing, nor does it address knowledge as politically organized.

I have argued that it is problematic to draw conclusions about the truth of women's ways of knowing without drawing attention to the politics of knowing. Despite extensive evidence that women do not learn easily in the context of male-designed educational models, and despite data which indicate a correlation between male abuse and women's difficulty in learning in male-dominated settings, the authors *naturalize* the assumption that women learn differently. From this naturalized position, and using the language of mothering, the authors argue that academic programs must be restructured to include this different way of knowing. Not addressed, however, is the way this view works to create yet another dualism: women as different. And not discussed is how an explicit theoretical validation of difference — an assumption implicit in mainstream curriculum and academic programming — might further disempower women in an educational system already failing to meet their needs, insofar as it is organized to reflect male experience and hence to entrench male power and authority. In this manner, the study obscures the question of how women's experiences are naturalized in the first place.

In this questionable shift — from women learn differently because of their experiences of male power and abuse of male power, to women learn differently because they are *naturally* different — the authors manage to locate/relocate the problems of why and how women find it difficult to learn within traditional educational settings squarely upon women's individual heads. Not considered are the social relations and structures which organize knowing and learning to prevent either women or men from seeing differently, and hence, changing. My resistance to this study is to a method of research which attempts to understand how women know by focusing on categories of knowledge that disconnect theory from social practice. Binding this theory of difference is a framework which could reproduce existing dominant educational practices. Without a politicized theory of knowing, which connects home practices to school practices, private practices to social practices, and which explicitly takes up theories of feminism, the model proposed by Belenky et al., despite its admirable attempt to validate women's maternal practices, cannot empower women: it does not begin from the explicit assumption that knowledge production is political activity developed to reproduce male academic forms.

It is commendable that Belenky et al. want to connect *being* and *knowing* through a model of education which draws from the everyday experiences of women whose lives are often organized by the work of mothering, which teaches much about the needs of others. It is even imaginable that such a model would benefit all of humankind. But surely if this model of education is to be workable, it must address more than the issue of difference — women's different ways of learning and knowing — in a society organized so predominantly by and for men. Theoretically, I am wary of a model of education based on *gender difference*. While it is important to continue considering new ways of moving ourselves beyond dualist modes of thought, as the authors attempt to do, I do not think it necessary to restrict these ways to an analytical framework defined either by maternal practices or by restrictive categorical ways of knowing, as in the educational work of Perry (1970), from whom these authors draw. What women's experiences indicate, however, are the limitations of current developmental and educational theory.

Implicitly, the work of Belenky et al. suggests a need for a major overhaul, rather than a *reshaping*, of current educational practices. This is an important text which enables us to think differently about women's ways of knowing. It stimulated me to begin examining the existing frameworks of education from my own perspective. The study raises questions worthy of serious consideration. It is a highly informative and compassionate work. Yet, to conclude that women know differently without theoretically analyzing how this is so, is, I think, to render invisible the practices which keep women's ways of knowing outside the state-legitimated educational institutions which inform knowing and learning. It is to perpetuate the traditional view of women as maternal care-givers and care-takers, without addressing the question of why men would want educational practices to work in any other way, when presumably they already work well to meet some men's needs. If we are going to take seriously Belenky et al.'s model based on notions of connection and caring, it must be appropriate to the educational needs of both women and men, a model which enables us to examine our assumptions about power, sexuality, gender, race and class.

Finally, I want to share with you a little story. Last week, when teaching a course entitled 'Sex Stratification', I found myself impatient and cranky with my students. I had been up late the night before and I was unusually tired. After several attempts to listen to and take seriously the concerns of one woman, who that day was monopolizing the class discussion, I could not stop myself from responding to her in an angry way. Subsequently, she jumped up and left the room in an equally angry manner. After some hesitation, I decided not to follow her, although I was not at all certain of what I should do. I began by apologizing to the class for my behaviour, explaining why I had responded in that manner. Discussion about class politics ensued. After assuring the class that I would arrange to discuss my behaviour with the woman who had left the class, and with assurances that we would take up the issue when she was present if she so chose, another woman in the class said something important to me:

> While we learn much from what you want to teach us, we also learn from what you do and don't do in the classroom. I think that it is good that we can get angry in the classroom.

I share this story with you because I am reminded of how much I was influenced as a student by teachers' practices, many of which are not included in the rubric of how we learn and know. In telling this story, I am reminded of teachers who have interacted with me in ways which have shaped and influenced how I learn. This kind of learning invites a bringing-together of body and mind, emotions and intellect. It invites honest reactions from both students and teachers. This means that since I as a teacher am struggling to develop safe learning spaces, I must also respond to the unexpected, including anger, in ways which will prove helpful (or at least not be intentionally destructive) to both myself and students. As a teacher I must struggle to develop consistency between my verbal and body languages. For victims of abuse, or for anyone, I would argue, this kind of body speaking, learning, and knowing always occurs. What is required, I suggest, is acknowledgment of this form of learning and knowing, in an academic context. I will speak more specifically about this in Chapter 5. Prior to this discussion, I intend in Chapter 4 to examine the relationship of *consciousness-raising* to teaching from a feminist perspective.

Love and Solidarity.

*Given my experiences as a woman, who learns both **inside** and **outside** structures of all kinds, I am wary of the theoretical divisions set up in the work of Belenky et al. In contrast to this inside/outside, dualistic theoretical approach to research, I want to begin from a different place,* *from which I can simultaneously celebrate difference and acknowledge inequalities. Unlike Belenky et al. who suggest that I can know about knowing, and know that theory is made from a focus on stages of knowing, I want to begin from the assumption that as knowledge is socially organized it is therefore necessary to focus on the ways in which subjects are organized to know. From this kind of knowledge we can learn to critique the values and assumptions which bind us to outmoded social practices. Autobiographical writings, I suggest, enable us to identify, analyze, and change those assumptions and social practices which work unconsciously to sustain social illusions.*

chapter four

A: Re-visioning through the Gaps and Cracks

Consciousness raising is a way of doing science, education and politics — it is a method that has been largely assumed, not problematized and not theorized... We need to learn ways of thinking how to integrate the personal and the political, the emotional and the intellectual in connection with consciousness raising. Without this, we can read texts that never touch us, that we can say apply to others, and claim that, in some way we have remained free of the impact of ideology and social regulation... I do not know if we can bring the method of consciousness raising into our academic work: I do not see how we cannot (Rockhill, 1986:18).

Reading and talking about reading with other women can change our perceptions of the world and help us to find the cracks in the walls of patriarchy that surround us... (Batsleer et al., 1985:154).

Buried or abandoned memories do not speak loudly... In recognition of this, we must adopt some method of analysis suited to the resolution of a key question for women; a method that seeks out the un-named, the silent and the absent (Haug et al., 1987:65).

Weedon (1987) suggests that we need to understand why women tolerate unequal relations of power (12). This is a question which keeps coming up in my discussions with battered women, as well as in my readings about male violence. Moreover, it is a question I now ask of my own social history. I think that, at one level, it is important to examine closely the more apparent social factors which work to make it easy for men in our society to violate women. At another is the problem of naming abusive practices which historically were considered to be the right of men: women were chattels of men. At this level, it is as difficult for women to find the **courage** to speak as it is to find the **words** to speak our abuses. Having been taught that our ordinary, everyday experiences are unimportant, we learn to dismiss the validity of these experiences. Often, our language does not provide the words to describe our experiences as women. This is because we live in a male-organized society in which language best describes the experiences of men. Thus, without the words and concepts to analyze abuse, it is understandable when we do not know we are abused. In fact, 'not knowing' is viewed as **natural** and **normal**. And yet, if this experience is really so natural and normal, why are we silent about our abuses? How do we learn to feel shame? Why does it take so much courage to speak of these abuses? What happens to us when we decide to tell? Having told, what do we do with our feelings of vulnerability? How do we recognize and what do we do with our feelings of guilt? Within academe? Within ourselves?

In Chapter 3 I began to theorize the relationship of feminist pedagogy to autobiography as method. In Chapter 5 I will discuss briefly how I began to learn and know differently as a result of my experiences in a women's consciousness-raising (CR) group. The skills I learned in this group I now bring to my teaching methods, especially with respect to taking up relations of power, sexuality, gender, race, and class. Despite these skills, my aim in Chapter 4 is to explicate, through narration, my difficulty in implementing these skills when confronting abusive situations. I think this difficulty is related to the fact that I learned, through abuse, to separate social practices into categories such as private and public for reasons of survival. In other words, what I did in CR I viewed as private and what I did in academe I viewed as public. My stories of abuse, of course, remained in the private category; they were even too private for the group. Because these kinds of separations are essential to the organization of education in a capitalistic, patriarchal society, it was difficult for me to view abuse as a social and political problem. Working from this perspective, it was almost impossible to name my abuse, because I had neither the language nor the support to do so. Only in the safety of CR groups could I begin to talk about my stories. Safety in the classroom takes much longer *to learn, I am discovering. I suggest, therefore, that it is the responsibility of teachers to help students begin to name that which has been silenced. This is a skill best learned in relation to others, in support networks. Whether or not we call such support groups CR groups is arbitrary, I suspect.*

Dear Lily, Andrew and Virginia:

For a variety of reasons, I have chosen to write this text in a letter format. Prior to the discussion I intend for Chapter 4, I want to pause for a moment and consider why I find it both helpful and creative to write in this mode. In many ways my reasons are really simple. On one hand, I find it difficult to write to an audience with whom I do not feel connected, even in an imaginary way. On the other hand, writing to such an audience allows me to imagine that we are in some way responsible to one another: me through writing and you through your responses.

Writing *as if* I can expect a response because I, in fact, invite response allows me to think of this work as part of ongoing research which is thus important not only because it will be a completed thesis but because of its continuing nature. Quite intentionally, I chose to organize my work in this manner for the purpose of disrupting a more traditional approach to producing a thesis, as well as to examine some of the illusory aspects of the more formal process. In effect, my aim in Chapter 4 is to explain why it is important to critique traditional academic forms, and at the same time address some of my assumptions about the relationship of consciousness-raising to feminist pedagogy.

I want to begin my letter today by noting my discomfort with an analytical distinction between the terms consciousness-raising and critical consciousness. In the past, I viewed consciousness-raising as an activity which happened outside the context of academic work. The purpose of CR was to receive and give support in a non-schooling context. I viewed critical consciousness as the activity of reading and writing in critical ways. Recently I have been considering the similarities between these two practices. In effect, both describe the process of learning to critique texts, whether the embodied text of self or the disembodied written text. Now that I understand these terms as describing a fundamental analysis of power, I am less inclined to note a difference. Supporting Rockhill (1986), I am increasingly interested in devising a critical pedagogy for both women and men based on the CR model.

I want to interrupt myself and note also my assumption that women-oriented spaces are crucial to the development of women's critical consciousness. Without the safety provided by a women's studies program, for example, I might not have found the strength to confront my abuse. For this reason, I praise scholars such as McIntyre (1986) and Rockhill (1986) who publicly speak and write about gender oppression. I mentioned to you in an earlier letter how Sheila's story about sexual harassment and Kathleen's story about sexual abuse provoked me to tell my stories.

Love and Solidarity.

B: Theorizing Memories

> We need a theory of the relation between language, subjectivity, social organization and power. We need to understand why women tolerate social relations which subordinate their interests to those of men and the mechanisms whereby women and men adopt particular discursive positions as representative of their interests (Weedon, 1987:12).

> Men **forget** their bodies; academic discourses are socially organized to deny (and/or deride) all bodies of history (and her-story) as *living* (Corrigan, 1987:1).

> I am born with short-comings for which I am responsible; eradicating them becomes my life's work. My very existence in the world becomes the potential source of a guilty conscience ... a question that arises from this is the extent to which a guilty conscience produced in this way provides fertile ground, or creates a readiness in us to subordinate ourselves to authority (Haug et al., 1987:39)?

Dear Lily, Andrew and Virginia:

So, why do women tolerate unequal relations of power? Why do I? As Weedon (1987) and Haug et al. (1987) note, this is not an easy question to answer. It is difficult precisely because of the ambiguities involved. Rarely, for example, as Haug et al. (1987) point out, do women live as either *victims* or as *active agents* who never again act in subordinate ways (145) upon recognition of how they are victims. Women, it seems, live "both dominance and subordination in one person..." (145). This being the case, Haug et al (1987) suggest that it is important theoretically to understand how and why women, in fact, live out the ambiguities of their contradictions (145).

For example, Haug and others demonstrate in their research, which is based on an analysis of their own stories, that while many women know themselves as active agents, it is apparent that these same women will learn to subordinate themselves to authority and power in a variety of ways and through a variety of means. Specifically, the authors suggest that women's very bodily "existence in the world can become a potential source of a guilty conscience" (128), a condition which can create "a readiness in women to subordinate themselves to authority" (128) despite a coexisting ability for the same women to act in more positive ways. For example, in the process whereby women actively, even willingly and enjoyably, take up social standards which define how their bodies should *look*, the potential to feel guilty is established simply because of the difficulties in meeting unrealistic standards; never quite thin enough is a prime example. The guilt produced by not being able to meet a given social standard, in this case what is perceived as necessary to achieve a particular look according to Haug et al. (1987), can prepare women for lives of subordination (145). Subordination here is dependent upon feelings of guilt produced when women are unable to reach a given social standard. It seems that guilt results even if the standard is unreasonable and unattainable for most women.

There is much about my own social history which suggests that I began to subordinate myself to figures of authority when I learned to internalize my feelings of guilt over being sexually abused. Over time any kind of abuse would produce the symptoms of subordination and guilt which I first learned through sexual abuse. Even now I continue to misread guilt as fear, danger, or loss of control: the feelings which most marked my early sexual abuse. Because I assumed as a child that it was I who was guilty and not my brother, I learned to forget the abuse. Thus I learned not to speak or name abuse. If, as he as the authority figure claimed, I was the guilty party, it is reasonable that I would not believe I had a valid story. After all, he was my older and well-respected brother. His status alone gave him authority. Who would believe me? By contrast, he was sure. He claimed his right. Anything else was a lie, he said. Somewhere mixed up in all of my responses was another kind of guilt. I imagined that my father loved me, but I also knew that he didn't appear to love my step-brother, Robbie. at some level I felt the injustice of this, and again internalized guilt for my brother's situation. Thus it was that I was denied access to my own authority as a speaker and writer. It is little wonder that for years I suffered fear of writing and speaking.

As an adult I still sometimes confuse fear, anger, rage, and guilt, and as a result sometimes respond to authority figures in ways which are not in keeping with my intentions. Often, it is only through more clearly manifested feelings of anger that I am able to then name and redirect my energy so as to meet my own needs rather than the needs of others. This whole process is particularly difficult, however, when authority figures (whether male or female) elicit fear (and defensiveness) in me for reasons I am not easily able to understand. Because of this I (still) sometimes attempt to absent or remove myself in a variety of ways. Ostensibly for reasons of survival, my intent is to escape feelings of fear rather than contend with interdependent feelings of fear, anger and guilt. Once I move into an escape or absentee mode, it becomes difficult, in this out-of-my-body experience, to sustain any sense of my own authority. In my imagination, however, I am in control because I am out-of-reach.

These are just a few examples of how I learned to tolerate unequal relations of power. There are others. These are some of the feelings and reactions I experienced as I lived the stories in Chapter 4. They are also some of the feelings and reactions I learned to identify and begin to change through my experiences in a *women's consciousness-raising group*.

Love and Solidarity.

C: In/forming Issues and Subjects

Women gained practical experience through consciousness-raising groups of retrieving from everyday life itself the means of transcending the everyday. It clearly boosted self-confidence to know that we were not alone in any of our various modes of experience; and yet there came a point at which we could progress no further. Telling stories became a circular process; no one wanted to listen any more. Hauling ourselves out of the water taught us nothing about flying, but a lot about gravity. As long as our experience was encased within obstinately repetitive gestures, it was impossible — since we had not yet begun to remember collectively . . . It was for this reason that we first proposed to work with and to theorize memory . . . We had to re-evaluate, to question what we had always taken for granted (Haug et al., 1987:39).

Dear Lily, Andrew and Virginia:

In my letter today I want to consider how I was affected by my experiences in a women's consciousness-raising group. My intent is to describe simultaneously the effects of this experience and how difficult it was for me to act upon my newly-felt feelings of power and control, especially as I confronted sexual harassment in an educational context.

I first knew the term *consciousness-raising* (CR) in the context of a small group of women who met on a weekly basis for the purpose of supporting one another. We adopted this term to both name our group and to describe the purpose of it (raising our individual and collective consciousness). As a result of this experience, I learned the validity of working in small groups. This is now a way of life for me. This was not always so.

I joined my first CR group in the late seventies, when I was attempting to cope with the contradictions, pleasures, and demands of the community in which I lived. For two years, I met with ten other women on a weekly basis. I was profoundly changed by our collective efforts to talk about, make conscious, and analyze, the impact of male dominance in our respective lives. As a result of this work I developed an increased respect for myself and for women generally. Through the experience, I came to know the power of a collective and politicized voice. I did not fully appreciate the extent to which a group method of examination would become a way of life.

The critical awareness I developed as a result of meeting with these women informed my life in alternating waves of exhilaration and chaos. In the safety of our group, I began to formulate new expectations of myself and of others, even though many topics remained taboo for me. This included discussions of body size or sexual abuse. Outside the group, my new awareness often met resistance in the everyday world. For example, one teacher told me that I was foolish to bring my "bullshit feminist analysis" into the classroom. My partner openly feared that I no longer *needed* him. Such responses worried me as I worked to merge my newly developing awareness with other social practices. During this struggle I began a Masters degree in anthropology. I was excited by the possibility of doing research which would relect my new interests.

Studying anthropology meant among other things that I could engage in field research. The idea of studying people's everyday experiences excited me. After completing a qualifying year, plus another year of course work, I decided I would do my field work in a shelter for battered women. This decision was inspired by an exchange I had with a male member of the department. Having just discovered the women's movement through my work in CR, I was angered by a comment he made in a graduate seminar. In response to questions about the comment, he announced emphatically that the women's movement was over, dead, a thing of the past. Puzzled by this pronouncement, I looked to the community for some sign that the movement was alive and well beyond the confines of one small CR group. My search to disprove his theory took me to a local shelter for battered women. I intended to use my research to learn about battered women and about this method of assisting them. I also wanted to check my perceptions of reality against his.

In talking with the women working in the shelter, I imagined that the existence of such a place was surely proof of a flourishing women's movement. Knowing little about shelter practices and even less about battering, I set out to examine the experiences of battered women. I naively assumed that my women-centred project would be of interest to the male members of my department, and to a few, in fact, it was. I had begun my work with the supportive words of my (male) advisor resounding in my ears: "I want to restate how much I think of this proposal and how innovative I think it is" (personal correspondence, 1981). Never, however, did I envision the multitude of problems which my naivete would provoke.

In retrospect, I was not emotionally and intellectually prepared, despite my developing self-awareness, for the resistance I met in writing and defending my thesis project. While experiencing difficulty in the department, I seldom considered my complaints and frustrations legitimate. More often I assumed that what I was feeling and experiencing was simply a product of being a graduate student. When I met with other women students in the anthropology department, we tended to talk about our work or about the feminist books we were reading outside of departmental requirements. We talked less about our frustrations as women students in a male-organized department. It was not until I neared completion of my thesis that a crisis occurred which resulted in a collective discussion and acknowledgement of our individual experiences. We discovered, for example, that a significant number of women students had been hurt and humiliated through experiences in this department. My aim in writing about this is to re-examine how I and others were disempowered by the social relations which organized our respective graduate school experiences. My express purpose is to *problematize* our collective experience.

D: Problematizing Experience: One Viewer Re-Viewing the Past

In consciousness-raising, new stories are born and women who hear and tell their stories are inspired to create new life possibilities for themselves and for all women (Christ, 1980:7).

Following others — schooling does not only teach subjects, it makes subjectivities (Corrigan, 1987:19).

I began my MA program with five other women and two men, all of whom, like myself, were privileged, white, middle-class students. Both men completed the program. Three women did not. The three women who did not finish were significantly hurt by their experiences, as were the three women who did complete the program.

In my case, I was verbally and emotionally abused by two males in the department. This not only affected me personally, but it also less directly affected my relationship with my thesis supervisor who, as an untenured member of the department, was caught in tensions which threatened his goal of becoming a legitimized, faculty member. In particular, I think he felt caught between his support for me and his need to please a powerful member of the department who considered my work with battered women to be unacceptable. In the words of this other individual, a topic such as battering was *too sensitive* a subject to constitute serious academic research. His assumptions about my work, gleaned only from reading the first three chapters of my thesis, resulted in a series of events which only later I learned to describe as abusive, violent and sexist.

Let me give you an example of how another student was treated in this department (by another professor). A graduate who was active in the department, an A student, and who also had chosen this department, in part, to accommodate family responsibilities, found herself having to work with a supervisor with whom she had difficulty due to differences in approach and personality. Despite these difficulties she completed her thesis. Her advisor refused to read it. Consequently, just prior to her intended defense date, the department had to find a reader from another university to read her thesis. While her work was highly rated, she quite understandably suffered as a result of this experience. The reasons for her advisor's withdrawal were never articulated to her. Despite the fact that both she and I were awarded external scholarships for work done in the department, we both initially doubted our academic abilities based on our respective experiences in this department.

The three women who left the program while I was doing my MA course work did not do so willingly. Because of a series of exchanges with persons in authority and for similarly unarticulated reasons, these women were forced to withdraw. One woman who had entered the program as an A student was requested by formal letter (a copy of which was put on her file) to leave the department because one professor considered her work unsatisfactory. Another woman, also an A student prior to admittance, was refused funding in the second year of her program. She was told that she had not made sufficient progress in her work. She argued that her progress in fact exceeded that of the two male students, who were receiving full funding. Without funds, she would be unable to commute the long distance to return to her family on weekends. One member of the department openly stated his resentment of her forthright manner, and told her that no faculty person was interested in or could supervise her work because of its esoteric quality: interested in medical anthropology, her aim was to study the health needs of women. Deflated by his comments and her inability to secure funding, she chose to leave the program. A third woman, initially funded for a two-year period, was refused further funding to complete her thesis. She, too, was dropped by her advisor, who openly expressed concern that her work had become *too feminist*. She quit the program. Doubting her abilities and frustrated that she was unable to include feminist readings in her research project, because of her advisor's adamant refusal to consider these readings, she chose to discontinue her program.

The one woman who did receive her degree somewhat unscathed by negative responses wrote a conventional non-feminist thesis about farming practices in the Netherlands. Politically astute about departmental politics and uninterested in a feminist perspective, and matched by interest with an advisor already somewhat marginalized in the department, she completed her degree without undue complication. Upon questioning later, however, she noted that she did not feel her work had been taken seriously by the men in the department. Nor did she feel that her thinking had been stretched by her work. The two male students graduated with honours.

I simply cannot write the anger I feel as I re-tell these stories. There is incredible sadness in knowing that the women of whom I speak initially perceived, internalized and privatized their experiences in this department. In part, the privatization occurred because we were leading active lives as partners, wives, mothers and women apart from the university. Many of us commuted fairly long distances. And, our outside interests acted to keep us somewhat uninformed of the others' problems. Additional factors silenced us. Each of us was differently afraid that we *couldn't make it* and unsure of our abilities at one level (though sure at another). We seldom spoke of our fears, especially with those with whom we were organized to compete for funding. Moreover, teaching and field research duties further separated and divided us.

When we finally came together as a political voice, following a crisis in which one woman refused to continue her silence about the treatment accorded her in this department, it was as women graduate students with little power, in a small department organized around male relations and interests. Brought together by this woman who decided to fight an unjust system, it was difficult for us to effect change for a variety of reasons. Most of us by this time had dispersed and were living or working in new communities. I, like some others, continued to doubt the legitimacy of my complaint. My insecurity and fear of authority figures, well learned as a victim of abuse, ultimately prevented me from protesting effectively.

Had a larger majority of us earlier recognized the political and theoretical complexities of our experiences, our eventual collective action might have had a greater impact than the minor administrative *hand slapping* which resulted from our action. Nonetheless, as a collective voice we related our individual stories to the dean of graduate studies who at the very least recorded them. Each of us was (individually) granted an interview set up by the dean's office. During my interview with the dean, a woman sympathetic to our stories, I was told that she too had suffered harassment several years earlier from which she was a long time recovering. The action which did result, however, could in no way compensate for the abuse suffered in this particular academic context.

Woven into this story of collective struggle is how I, as an individual, did and did not take up the abuse I had experienced in this department. My difficulties were in no way explicit in my thesis about battered women. Basically, I constructed a thesis which reflected my need to produce a work acceptable to the male-organized department. Given continued support from my supervisor, I was not prepared for the way in which he responded to my research during the final stages of my program. For example, in a long and detailed letter he wrote:

> In sum, I find that the Transition House conclusion that battering is a logical deduction from hierarchical relationships to be a faulty one, and their remedy — the radical re-structuring of social relationships — an unrealistic (and unnecessary) utopian dream. You must make a clear distinction between you as analyst reporting Transition House ideology and you as advocate (or non-advocate). If it appears to the reader that you accept Transition House ideology, and/or are pushing it, I fear the consequences (personal correspondence, 1982).

For certain, he was correct in assuming that I had taken an ideological stance. Unfortunately, I did not know then that I was working from my own *preferred* ideological perspective. I assumed at one level that I knew the truth of the situation. I was convinced that the work of shelters was politically organized to teach women to live in the world differently: to teach them how and why they did not need to accept violence. This difference, I assumed, required a radical restructuring of relationships. I wanted to convince my advisor of this *truth*. That we were both working from vested interests in specific ideological perspectives was not then clear to me. We entered into a battle of positions, he arguing that a radical restructuring was not necessary, and I arguing that it was. While I would still argue that a radical restructuring of society is necessary, I am now able to understand my position as a (preferred) perspective and not as the truth. I do not know if he learned this difference. This story is yet another example of how I am coming to understand knowledge as socially constructed.

In the letter from which I just quoted, my advisor also criticized me for discussing the limitations of the theoretical approach I was using. In his opinion, talking about limitations was indicative of weaknesses in the work. In view of his comments, and despite his assurance that my thesis was acceptable, I reluctantly prepared for my defense.

My MA defense was two and one-half hours long. My topic was criticized, as was my ability to be objective. One member of the department suggested that for me to study the lives of battered women would be like him studying Alcoholics Anonymous. In other words, because he is an alcoholic, his personal involvement precludes his writing about it. Despite my assurance that I was not a battered woman (as I then understood the term), his experience was considered sufficient reason for me not taking up this kind of work.

Just prior to the actual defense, a member of the department asked my advisor — who immediately related the comment to me — whether "the dykes from the House would be at the defense to protect?" During my defense the chair of my committee also put this sentiment into written form. As I mentioned earlier, the note in which he expressed his homophobia was left in a copy of my thesis and returned to me. My advisor, then untenured, was reluctant to address, despite his stated disapproval, the contents of this note or the manner in which the defense had been conducted. Instead, he congratulated me on completion of a good thesis. The chair of my committee said nothing. On file was a letter expressing his disapproval of my work.

For weeks following this event I could not talk about my feelings. It has taken me years to make sense of what happened in that small department of anthropology. I left the study of anthropology, in part, because of this experience. Although I confronted some of the abuse while still in the department, much was left unsaid and unnamed. Some of it I simply ignored in order to survive. Only much later, through investigation and in talking with other women, was I able to see the bigger patterns of abuse which organized my experiences and those of other women students. While some of what we experienced is directly related to the needs of one individual who wielded much power in a network of social relations, much is also directly attributable to the immense support of the men who condoned his actions.

I felt considerable helplessness in understanding the behaviour of many of the men in the department. My responses were complicated by the fact that I knew my teachers outside the university context. My children attended schools with their children. Most of all, I simply did not understand the way in which the abuse unfolded. Not understanding, I directed my anger inward, fearing that I did not deserve better treatment. I felt guilty because I was 'unable' to produce an *objective* thesis.

Despite the fact that I did confront some of the abuse as it occurred, confrontations always took place at the expense of my emotional and physical well-being. In many ways, each was an emotional re-enactment of the sexual abuse I had endured as a child. In fearful situations, I (sometimes) feel the abuse at a deep bodily level. To avoid such responses is difficult. It requires considerable energy and a kind of support seldom provided in non-woman-centred schooling contexts. From my particular schooling experience, and those of other women, I learned much about power, pain, violence and humiliation. Lacking helpful thesis supervision, I did not, however, learn about a very real theoretical problem in my academic work.

E: Re-visioning Anew

If the reader merely wants to use the findings of the authority in his (sic) ordinary human relations, he will find himself sooner or later in an argument in which he hurls his authority at some one else's head and gets some one else's authority hurled back at him . . . I should like . . . to do more than this. I should like to be able to interpose between my statement and the reader's consideration of the statement a pause, a realization not of what authoritative right I have to make the statement I make, but instead of how it was arrived at, of what the anthropological process is (Mead, 1949:35).

About a year-and-a-half ago, I vividly lived and wrote through a very dark period in my life when I finally

> broke the cycle of abuse that I had been locked into for nearly 40 years. In going back over the material, I came to see the extent to which my head was central to how I'd reproduced my abuse. To briefly explain, had you ever asked me what I thought was crucial to the development of critical consciousness, I would have responded that it was understanding how we are socially constructed. I had an intellectual understanding of my oppression that in a very bizarre way made it possible for me to reproduce it... (Rockhill, 1986:13).

> Must we observe the golden rule of pedagogy, and withhold from others what has been withheld from us? And if teaching the text calls on us to struggle for the ownership of meaning with our own parents, wouldn't it be decent to confess that they are the ones we see when we lean across the podium to teach the twenty year olds who are our students (Grumet, 1985:17)?

I first sensed a theoretical problem in my MA work when attempting to critique my advisor's assumption that I was in difficulty as an academic because I had accepted transition house ideology. He was correct to ask me to make a clear distinction between myself as analyst and myself as analyst with a preferred ideological preference, but he did so, I suggest, without fully taking into account the implications of his own ideological preference. From his comments, it is (now) apparent that he did not perceive himself as working from a preferred ideological stance. However, from this stance and from his position of power and authority, he was able to organize the ensuing battle lines with him on one hand, explicitly arguing for the maintenance of the status quo, and me on the other, arguing for a radical restructuring of social relations. Exercising his power, he rigidly bound us both to an either/or defensive theoretical position. Either he was right and I was wrong, or he was wrong and I was right. Unable to guide me, or me him, to a place where we could see how we were both bound by our ideological perspectives, we entered a power struggle that I, and presumably he, did not theoretically or emotionally comprehend. Only years later, when I began to understand knowledge as socially organized and constructed, did I begin to see how we were similarly bound by our respective notions of truth and our either/or ideological perspectives, and by the *differential relations of power* which divided us as teacher and student.

Understanding the basis of this kind of power struggle only partially lessens the pain of the actual experience. Through description and analysis I use these stories to demonstrate how specific academic experiences damaged me. I aim also to demonstrate how the women with whom I began my graduate studies were damaged by schooling practices. I use these stories to show how specific figures of authority reproduced in me feelings of fear and guilt which prevented me from acting in a more direct and less personally damaging manner. However, in retelling these stories I am beginning to more fully recognize the connections between how I learned to fear authority figures and how I subsequently learned to tolerate unequal relations of power.

Given the basis of our stories, I no longer believe it is good enough to conclude that women are able to acquire knowledge in-spite-of, or because of, pain incurred in the process of doing graduate work. Clearly, this pain must be analyzed and related to the sexist practices which organize our experiences and not, as Belenky et al. (1986) might suggest, from the view that women essentially work from a non-politicized *different way of knowing*. What I'm arguing for here is the *problematizing of experience* in order to comprehend how women's subjective experiences are organized by specific social practices and thereafter affirmed by gender-specific schooling practices which work to benefit men more than women. From a focus on my experience of doing graduate work in one university, my aim is to suggest, through description and analysis, how women are socially organized to know in particular ways. I suggest this kind of organization is similar to the way that women are organized to know abuse in a family context.

To talk about women's different ways of knowing, as do Belenky et al. (1986), apart from a critique of knowledge as socially organized through experience, and apart from analysis of male power and abuse, is to perpetuate a way of thinking about knowledge production which does not allow for social or individual change or difference. This way, I think, forces learners to unconsciously repeat cycles of organizing knowledge that work to silence women. It is this manner of writing, and this way of writing about knowledge, that I am attempting to disrupt and change through the process of autobiographical reflection and analysis.

I began this story with an introduction to my experience of CR because it was from there that I began to question in a theoretical way, how and why women tolerate unequal relations of power. It was in this group that I began to feel safe enough to question male authority in a public context. There my stories seemed neither strange nor crazy. This experience enabled me to seriously examine my private fears. There, we began to collectively and individually theorize our memories. Moving this analysis from the safety of the group to less safe public discourses was difficult. Many of us assumed a split between the kinds of (private) knowledge that we spoke freely of in our CR groups and the kinds of (public) knowledge we had to produce and reproduce socially, despite our efforts to recognize the importance of such splits.

I think it was my early work in CR which provided me with skills for naming and recognizing my own reactions, assumptions and responses. These skills now shape my teaching practices. The CR experience has enabled me to explore and disrupt many of the traditional methods of learning which organized my schooling practices for so long. Whether CR occurs in writings, within the classroom, at home, or in one-to-one relationships, it continues to enable me to name and re-name my subjective experience as a woman academic. As such, this method of naming experience in the form of stories which are then critiqued is an important theoretical practice.

I discovered through teaching that the public speaking skills I learned in my CR group, and some of the skills I learned in therapy, are vital to my classroom practices. These skills enable me to examine with my students how we are differently shaped by the relations of power which organize our lives. When anger, frustration, fear, and happiness erupt as a result of seeing the world differently through critique, I am discovering it is helpful to draw from experiences which teach me not to fear those eruptions (Williamson, 1981/82).

These are skills, I suggest, which must be learned if we as educators are truly committed to bringing new issues, such as abuse, into curricula. Further, I think this awareness must be learned if we are to bring about any kind of change. I use these skills, for example, when I work with a student who has completed three years of university and cannot yet imagine what work she would like to do. When she begins to recognize, through her writings and readings, that her assumptions about marriage and motherhood are related to her inability to seriously consider a career, her anger emerges and needs to be addressed. The anger young men express when I ask them to write about male violence from the perspective of a violator is stressful both for the writer and for me. To explicitly take up problems of power, sexuality, gender, race, and class is difficult work and, I think, demands an awareness that graduate students are seldom taught. Without understanding the struggle in this kind of work, it is difficult to bring together theory and practice in a learning context.

I think there is a major difference between acquiring skills for the purpose of guiding students through their own writing experiences and the experience of *doing therapy*. What I do in the classroom when I examine how gender relations are socially constructed, for example, may in fact be therapeutic for students, but this does not mean that I am doing therapy. My role is not that of a therapist. Like a good therapist, however, I do ask questions of the material presented to me and I do teach students to ask questions in their writing and reading. I attempt to teach them to view critically their work, their assumptions, and their theories as socially constructed either by themselves or by others. That they feel better in the process is, of course, therapeutic.

Key to my work is teaching students to see how assumptions about sexuality, power, gender, race, and class are at work both in their own texts and in the texts of others. For students and teachers to do this kind of work is what Aiken et al. refer to as a dual task, "to rethink the role of gender within their disciplines and to interrogate the very structures on which their disciplines were erected" (1987:259). Seeing this is often resisted (Aiken et al., 1987). Changes are difficult. It is also a way of seeing that sometimes brings out the buried or abandoned memories we have been taught as students (and teachers) to hide, repress, or ignore through formal schooling practices. Once out, however, we as teachers (and students) must learn to take responsibility for our memories, else we again teach silence.

As Haug et al. so aptly state in their analysis of sexuality as a form of socialization (25), "Buried or abandoned memories do not speak loudly" (65). Rather, we must find and create words to describe that which is not easily accessible. In constructing a language to describe the abuses which we as women live, we can begin to better understand ourselves and the social practices which shape our lives. From this understanding, we can analyze the very material basis of language, which until recently has not allowed us to write or speak our abuses.

Love and Solidarity.

Once we write and speak our abuses publicly, thereby entering them into the dominant public discourses, we can begin to see language as malleable and socially constructed. In this way we can theorize women's abuse and, through language practices, re-define and re-mold the previously un-named, the silences which worked so effectively to shape and reproduce our abuses. In making public our abuses, we also begin to theorize and alter the language practices which have kept this violence in the realm of the private, the individual and the fixed. In writing of our abuses, we can create new theories to explain this abuse. In this manner, buried memories become the material of theory (Haug, 1987).

chapter five

A: Glimmerings into the Dark

Children have two visions, the inner and the outer. Of the two the inner vision is brighter (Ashton-Warner, 1983:32).

I could not have learned that I was worth caring for from one who did not celebrate her own worth (Spring, 1987:65-66).

In Chapters 1 through 4, I introduced and analyzed a number of autobiographical stories I believe are key to my social formation. In Chapters 5 through 7 I will work with another form of autobiographical data: papers I wrote as a graduate student. In this section, each chapter has as its focus an essay completed prior to my decision to write about my abuse. I chose the three papers used in these chapters because they represent the emergence from silence about my abuse. While I was not prepared to speak about the abuse at the time of writing, in retrospect I see myself being readied to confront my abuse. I view these papers as a kind of journal representing either a shift in my learning or a place of feeling stuck; and alternately, a moment of recognition. Methodologically, I use them as stories from which to further analyze the patterns of abuse which inform how I do or do not learn in a given context. Following Haug et al. (1987), the method of re-learning which I use to critique these stories involves "seeing what is not said as interesting, and the fact that it was not said as important; it involves a huge methodological leap and demands more than a little imagination" (65). I begin this critique from my assumption that essays, like stories, are at once autobiographical and theoretical.

Chapter 5 is important because it narrates how I understand that knowledge is socially constructed. In this chapter I examine how abuse worked to damage my inner visions. Woven through this analysis is a brief introduction to the work of Ashton-Warner (1963), whose notion of **key words** *I use to examine the assumptions which organized my first reading of Virginia Woolf's (1938) essay on education.*

> First words must mean something to a child. First words must have intense meaning for a child. They must be part of his (sic) being (Ashton-Warner, 1963:33).

Dear Lily, Andrew and Virginia:

In her work with Maori children in New Zealand, Ashton-Warner (1963) devised a method of teaching young children to read and write. Central to this method is the assumption that children bring to their early learning two visions: an *inner* and an *outer*; the inner being the brighter of the two, located as it is in the everyday experience of the child (32). In her opinion, organic learning occurs when the first words a child learns mean something to her or him (33). Problematic for Maori children is learning in a context in which they must re-translate the experience of being black into the language experience of the dominant white culture. Thus, explicit in Ashton-Warner's work is the assumption that racial differences result in Maori children not being able to learn their own key vocabulary. Instead, they are compelled to learn the vocabulary of a dominant white culture. Therefore, unless Maori children are taught otherwise, they will learn to read, write and speak not from an inner vision but from an outer vision located outside Maori experience. In this manner, Maori children will learn to read in a rote, rather than an organic, manner (1963).

Ashton-Warner's analysis could apply to women like myself who are taught to read and write in a culture founded upon the literary expertise of the dominant white male experience. Furthermore, I would suggest that young girls entering into the dominant language practices of such a culture are taught to translate from their experience as young women to the male norm where, of course, they will not fit because they are not boys or men. This process of translation is described well by Smith when she writes about women entering into a "male world in its assumptions, its language, its patterns of relating. The intellectual world spread out before me appears, indeed I experienced it, as genderless" (1987:7).

For women like myself who are abused at an early age, entry into language practices can be doubly difficult. Not only must we begin the process of translating our experience to fit with the dominant model, but we must do this from a damaged inner vision. In my case it was almost impossible to learn to speak and write from an inner vision I had learned to distrust. It had been damaged by my brother's abuse. And, because I could not talk about this abuse, I learned to distrust my key words: I could not trust what I could not speak. Through fear I learned to deny my key words and my key experiences. I think any woman or girl taught to translate her experience is, in fact, learning to work from a damaged inner vision.

As a survivor of incest, my entry into language was confusing. For example, I entered reading with a vigour bordering on compulsion. Reading was a pleasure because it enabled me to hide, to escape from my memory of abuse. It allowed me to imagine a better world than the one I knew. Writing, however, was not a pleasure and for many years I did not understand how I could be a competent reader and an incompetent writer (I make reference to this incompetence in several places in this text). Feeling incompetent, it is not surprising that I searched for a 'perfect' methodology which would enable me to 'get it right', to be 'objective' from a male perspective.

My search to find the perfect methodology shifted most dramatically when, in my forties, I began to write about my experience of abuse. It is this writing which enables me to understand the relationship between my inability to speak my abuse and my inability to write. I could not write because I feared what might come out. At the age of thirteen this fear became a symptom: my hand hurt when I wrote. Even now I hold my hand in a pained and contorted way when I hand-write. I used to interpret this pain as my intellectual inability to write an essay.

For many years I did not connect my inability to write an essay with a critique of the difficulties I experienced when writing in a male-organized culture. Without having learned to critique relations of power from a feminist perspective, how could I? Instead I suffered through classroom experiences wherein I found myself listening to teachers who told me to believe their words, to believe in ideals such as equality, freedom, and justice for all. As an abuse survivor, I knew I was neither free nor equal and I did not feel the world was just. Because I could not speak this knowledge, I learned how dangerous writing could be. I learned, too, to distrust the words of authorities (this may have allowed me to survive) in their espousal of ideals I knew as lies. Yet, I remained caught in the contradiction of having learned to distrust authority figures while distrusting my own self-authority, lost as it was through abuse.

The knowledge that I did not have real access to power and authority as defined by cultural norms resulted in choosing (somewhat consciously) during my teen years to 'get it over with', to become what I assumed was expected of me. If what was expected was to become a wife and mother, then why wait? Why wait and pretend I was important enough to seriously think I might study or choose a career? Abuse having taught me to see myself through others' eyes, I found it difficult to see myself through my own eyes, even though I continued to resist the power of 'those' authority figures (i.e. my brother) 'out there', whom I did not really believe. After all, I knew my brother's power and authority, at another level, to be a lie. I think knowing this enabled me to survive. To move beyond my victim practices is more difficult.

In Chapter 1, I talked about the shifts which enabled me to define myself other than as *victim*. I think my decision to move to an academic environment in which I could theorize male violence from a feminist perspective was the most significant event marking my shift from victim to survivor. Not only did this environment provide a context for analyzing male violence but, as importantly, it felt safer than all my previous academic environments had. Here I began to take seriously a desire to bring together, theoretically and practically, my private and public feminist practices.

Initially, I felt overwhelmed by the energy, creativity, brilliance, support, care, conflict, and honesty of this environment organized to support scholars working from feminist perspectives. I delighted in my immersion in texts I had previously considered my private reading. It was exciting to work with instructors who encouraged me to examine my own experience while critiquing theory, whether in fiction or essay form.

In this environment I felt like a child discovering the world. Like the children taught by Ashton-Warner (1963), I experienced the joy of working with teachers who encouraged me to examine my inner visions and to write using my key vocabulary (32), though this practice was not named as such. How surprising it was to discover that teachers did not expect me to reproduce the outer male visions. However, because I had learned well to reproduce my visions in a world which teaches women that the things we experience are "unimportant and uninteresting" (Haug et al., 1987:38), at first I found it difficult to transgress these boundaries and write creatively from my perspective as a woman.

Because I had learned to survive through reading fictional accounts, it was important to experience classroom situations in which I could work with multi-varied texts, including the text of self. Specifically, however, fictional accounts are important to me because as a genre they are not intentionally set up to convince readers of how the world should be organized. While novels may work in this manner, they are written to encourage reader response and interpretation. In this way novels enable readers to imagine new and creative ways of thinking about the world.

Fictional accounts are important, I know from experience, because they excite the imagination and emotions. From this place we feel free to imagine and to create new possibilities. For abuse survivors this is important because we may be stuck in the trauma of the abuse and in need of ways to imagine becoming unstuck. In recent years I have experienced a similar kind of excitement in reading feminist theory. I do not wish to imply, however, that I never experience rapport with male-constructed theory. I do. There is however, a difference.

Based on my reading of feminist writers who theorize the everyday experience of women, I am discovering a correlation between theory as academically defined and theory as produced in fiction. Importantly, I am finding that theory which takes into account women's everyday experiences, as fiction does, also ignites emotion and imagination. From here I can better understand theory as ideologically and socially constructed. Out of this discovery, I am beginning to imagine how to more consciously work with these two modes — fiction and theory — as tools for effecting recognition (hence change) of how texts organize readers in specific ways: each in their own way both theoretical and fictional. This use was described in Chapter 3. But I am getting somewhat ahead of myself because, in fact, this discovery came later than that which I introduce here.

I am about to introduce a paper I wrote while a graduate student. I completed this piece just prior to my decision to write about my experiences of abuse. Importantly, I could neither complete my thesis nor do the work of teaching until I wrote my abuse stories. I feared facing students because of the shame I felt. In retrospect, I think my reading of Woolf's (1938) text, and my subsequent decision to use it as the basis for a paper, is connected to my preparedness to write about abuse. How so?

I believe I chose to work with Woolf's text *Three Guineas* (1938) because it provided a *point of reference* from which to retrospectively examine my preparations for confronting the abuse. This understanding is, of course, current. I did not have it at the time of writing the paper.

I recall well reading *Three Guineas* (1938) for the first time. In particular, I recall the excitement I felt when I first encountered the term *absenting* in Woolf's (1938) text. I was delighted by Woolf's term to describe how women could re-claim power in a male-organized society simply by 'removing' themselves from unpleasant situations. During this early reading, however, I was not thinking about myself needing to re-claim power. Rather, I was concerned about battered women. I wanted to know how this term could be applied to the conditions of their lives.

From the perspective of Sylvia Ashton-Warner's (1963) work, it is clear to me now that the term *absenting* was a word in my key vocabulary

(32). At an unconscious level, I am certain I was drawn to it because it so aptly described a practice I knew as a survivor of abuse. For example, I knew well how to absent myself in my reading practices, though at the time I had not connected this to abuse. I understood less about the ways I absented myself when fearful, though I knew the consequences of my actions.

The text was also important to me because it provided, in novel form, a critique of male-organized educational practices. At the time of first reading this text, however, I did not have a conscious awareness of my desire to teach or my fear of teaching. In fact, when I read and enjoyed any critique of educational practices, such as that in Woolf's (1938) text, I assumed they were important to me because I had so disliked most of my schooling experience prior to university, while contradictorily loving learning. Never had I connected the absence of enjoyment, or a need to critique, to abuse.

Lastly, it is important to note that prior to reading Woolf's (1938) account, I was unable to finish any of her other novels. On many occasions I had attempted to do so. This was because each of my readings evoked a kind of fear in me. Only in hindsight do I know my fear was related to the fact that many of Woolf's accounts contain her attempts to write about and analyze her own experiences of abuse (see for example DeSalvo's (1989) excellent book). Thus, I avoided Woolf's texts because I could not bear to read about abuse, not having confronted my own. In fact, not until I began to write about my abuse could I read about the experiences of other women. I think this fear could have been addressed much sooner had I worked with feminist teachers knowledgeable about the effects of abuse on women readers.

When I later related my love of this text to my thesis supervisor, she asked me to explain what it was about Woolf's account which "brought me in" and "how was it that my experience of reading this account seemed to open a window through which I could see something"? Her questions are good ones. They are the questions of a helpful teacher and reader. She did not, for example, attempt to tell me what I saw. Rather, she asked questions which stimulated me to delve deeply into my own experience, from my own perspective. More specifically, this advisor noted two aspects of my initial attempts to understand the importance of the text to me. One, she prompted me to consider further why the term *absenting* seems to be key for me; and, two, she asked me to consider why she felt as though I were not in the text despite the fact that I often spoke in the first person. Her comments were crucial, I think, to the shift I was making. They inspired me to consider further what I am actually saying when I claim to be unable to write essays. What do I mean?

What I mean when I say I am unable to write essays is that although the thinking I do for essays is derived from an inner vision (this I have always felt confident about), when I begin putting these thoughts into writing I rely on external rather than internal authority because, in fact, I am *translating*. I am writing to make my words fit a vision which is not mine. Moreover, I must translate twice, once as a victim of abuse, and once as a woman. In both cases it is difficult then to process information (a socially constructed vocabulary) with my inner key words through which I interpret the social world. I am not implying here that these are two realities but, rather, I remind readers (and myself) that it is always individuals (with differing perspectives) who take up language constructions in a social way. Not easily able to pass this language through my own perspective as both a victim and woman, I sometimes produce works in which I am absent (at one level). At another, I produce essays.

What being absent means, therefore, is that I do not work from a perspective, framework, or authority which is mine. Rather, I work from that of the person or audience for whom I am writing, whether real or imagined. Interestingly, Dorothy Smith drew my attention to this habit two years before I was able to comprehend or appreciate the significance of her words, when she noted my tendency to "hide myself in my written texts". In retrospect, I was unable to comprehend Smith's analysis earlier because I had not begun my own analysis of how abuse had affected me.

It was not until after I had written about myself as a survivor of abuse that I understood fully my attraction to the term *absent*. The images presented by this word were initially much too frightening and reminded me at a less conscious level of how abuse had taught me to absent myself, especially in fearful situations. The term, I knew only too well, described what I had learned to do as a means of survival. In the early stages of remembering, as I began to understand why the term was key for me, I did not perceive it to be positive with regard to my own experience. I saw it as a positive term only for battered women. I did not want to be reminded that I was a survivor, and in fact, most of my conscious memories of abuse were buried. I wanted to forget. Recalling abuse is fearful. As suggested in the work of Ashton-Warner my key word was buried deep in both "fear" and "sex" (1963:42). Once I began to examine the memories which this word evoked, I too began a long and difficult recovery process.

Like the children of Ashton-Warner's (1963) classroom, I sensed my need to work with teachers who were strong in themselves in order to begin examining my own traumas. This was because I knew well the experience of telling 'unacceptable' stories to teachers who are not strong. As you know the reaction is sometimes one of horror: it is rather like homophobia, where people fear for themselves rather than the victims. In a schooling context, this kind of response is damaging; it reaffirms the bad feelings which the victim knows only too well.

In retrospect, I think I began to confront the key term *absenting* in this particular essay, in this particular classroom, at this particular time, in part because I felt safe enough to do so. I think, too, that it was important I was in analysis. At the same time, I felt myself safe, surrounded by a network of women friends, supporters and teachers committed to feminism, social critique, and social change.

The teacher for whom I wrote the following paper is a woman I respect. She taught me much about teaching. Not only did I enjoy her presentation of self but I regard highly her teaching practices. Apart from being an active, interested, and interesting teacher and scholar, she listened well to the concerns and questions of students in her classroom. Her eyes listened, as did her body. She let us see her as a person, hence we became persons to her. From her approach, I re-learned, as I have from a few others, what it means to be a good teacher: someone who can help develop students' skills from a place of inner and outer vision.

It was difficult to re-read the essay I chose for this chapter. Theoretically, I make lots of leaps and jumps which demand considerable work from readers. (But, why not?) The instructor who graded this paper was very fair, I think. Rather than focusing on the weaknesses of the paper, she very astutely looked for the (often hidden) strengths. In particular, she encouraged my imaginative attempts to show how the ideas in Virginia Woolf's (1938) text are socially relevant. In grading this essay, I suspect she worked to view it in the larger context of other papers I was expected to do for the course, rather than focusing on the limitations of this particular piece.

> Back to these first words. To these first books. They must be made out of the stuff of the child itself (Ashton-Warner, 1963:34).

> Language can serve either as a prison, or as the material of liberation (Haug et al., 1987:36).

I would ask that you read the following essay with the above comments in mind. For me, this essay is but one form of data from which I examine how my learning was affected by abuse. Specifically, I ask that you keep in mind, as you read, that which I do not include in the writing.

Love and Solidarity.

B: Peace and War: Absenting the Subject

<Essay One>

Mead (1984) suggests that warfare was invented by men for the purpose of accumulating loot, territory, wives, and other forms of property which might be of value to them (133). Noting this, she implores her readers to consider alternatives to war, stressing that as with other outmoded inventions, something must be invented to replace it (134). While I agree wholeheartedly with Mead's sentiment, I also know how difficult it is to replace old ways with new ones.

Warfaring is a long-standing traditional means of organizing and controlling social and economic relations. Woolf's treatise (1938) ably demonstrates why an extreme exercising of both will and imagination is required to develop alternative ways of organizing education which will better serve the needs of women and men. In my opinion, Virginia Woolf has achieved this in her excellent treatise on education. Based on my reading of Woolf's text, my intent is to explicate in a two-part paper my belief that she has written a treatise on peace and not, as is often assumed, a treatise on war.

In imagining the development of alternative educational institutions, I am intrigued by the work of Franklin (1984) who has devised a way of considering new possibilities through a practice she calls *imaging*. This method of doing science is different from the usual scientific method of reaching a goal by forecasting or projecting a certain known variable into the future along a linear time line. In contrast to the method of advance forecasting, Franklin suggests researchers *image* a desired goal, imagine how it might look and proceed by *projecting back* the resources and constraints involved in effecting the goal (88). She argues that this method is less restrictive than the forecasting techniques used by many scientists. *Imaging* therefore provides a space for researchers to generate the kinds of questions and answers necessary to end warfaring as a means of social control. It is this method of *imaging* which I will use to organize my reading of Woolf's *Three Guineas* (1938). I use this method to examine Woolf's discussion of how to effect peace rather than support war.

In reading Woolf's account, I am intrigued by her use of a concept she refers to as *absenting*. Specifically, she develops the concept for the purpose of showing women how they might remove or absent themselves from male-organized methods of control. In particular, Woolf is interested in the concept of *absenting* because she views it as a practical technique for women to remove themselves from negative situations. From her perspective, absenting would enable women to use their imaginations to stop being complicit in negative situations; in particular, it would enable them to register radical disapproval. I think, therefore, that this technique deserves serious analysis, both in its imaginary worth and in its potential practical worth.

Like Franklin's imaging technique, to absent oneself from the status quo is, I suggest, one means of survival used by feminists in a variety of ways. For example, based on my experience with transition house workers, I suspect that the movement to provide battered women with special housing was initiated because women used their imaginations to absent themselves from the status quo perception of wife battering as a social norm. Once removed, women involved in the shelter movement were able to imagine a new way of assisting battered women. Similarly, I suggest, men must remove themselves from warfare in order to imagine other ways of ordering society.

It is common for people to think of war as a peace-keeping activity rather than a war-making activity. My intent in this paper is to discuss the unique contribution which Woolf makes to the analysis of peace, in the context of discussing war. I will focus on the ways in which Woolf's text (1938) explicates how women can physically and psychologically absent themselves from outmoded social structures which support war. From this focus, I will discuss why *Three Guineas* is an account focused on peace rather than war. I differentiate between notions of *peace-making* and *peace-keeping* for the purpose of discussing why I think war is a war-making activity, not a peace-keeping activity.

Peace-keeping is still traditionally practised by women within the confines of home-making. It is likely that such a skill was developed by women for the explicit purpose of coping with the practices which support male power, particularly as practised by males who, as *heads of households*, are able to exercise considerable power over women. On a broader scale outside the home, men who are interested in warfare activities are often considered to be peace-keepers. In more recent years, particularly with the development of the women's movement, women are beginning to critique the male belief in war as a means of keeping peace. Rather than ignore issues of war, however, women are devising new ways of making peace at both the home and global level. Similarly, groups of women are expressing dissatisfaction with the idea of keeping peace in the home simply for the sake of peace.

For example, battered women are refusing to accept male abuse and, with the support of women's shelters, are choosing to absent themselves from homes in which abuse is practised. Through making such choices, women are beginning to perceive themselves as agents of social change in a larger sense. In this manner women are organizing to make peace rather than to keep peace, an active rather than a passive stance.

The idea of conscious peace-making, which differs from the more traditional peace-keeping, is one which I first encountered while doing research in a transition house for battered women. Rather than attempt to keep peace in the context in which they are violated, battered women have begun to remove themselves from their homes and from abusive situations. The decision to absent themselves from male abuse and to seek help from the women residing or working in transition houses is supported and validated by other positive experiences in shelters.

For example, in the collectively-organized house most familiar to me, battered women are encouraged to initiate change from the perspective of their own needs rather than the needs of the men who batter them. In this way, battered women come to view themselves as social activists. In absenting themselves from the battering, women simultaneously absent themselves from dependency upon a batterer's decision to, or not to, change. Thus, irrespective of a batterer's decision to change, some battered women are learning to access their own power by leaving intolerable situations and making peace for themselves. Instead of working to keep peace (at expense to themselves) for the purpose of sustaining an ideal image of home and family, women who absent themselves can begin to imagine creative alternatives. In a similar manner, women's peace groups are creating new ways of organizing peace.

Strategies designed to eliminate oppressive gender relations, whether in a family or broader social context, are often perceived as hostile. Gilbert, for example, implies that Woolf is hostile in her presentation of men,

> It is in Virginia Woolf's *Three Guineas*, the postwar era's great text of pacifist feminism, that such hostility to men comes most dramatically to the surface in the form of violent anti-patriarchal fantasies paradoxically embedded in an ostensibly nonviolent treatise on the subject of "how to prevent war" (1983:445).

Gilbert's conclusion that Woolf's treatise is a violent, hostile, antipatriarchal fantasy is an interesting one which, I think, prevents her from seeing the specific genius of Woolf's work. Gilbert's interpretation does not allow her to see how Woolf imagines a new kind of society or that, through the imaginative use of questions, she is able to critique state and patriarchal power. And, as Warnock so aptly points out, "The power of patriarchy is such that to see through it requires a special kind of vision, a consciousness of the most **ordinary** experience" (1982:28).

As Woolf's work demonstrates, it is necessary to critique all forms of oppression, and with courage and vision to imagine new ways of organizing society. Such is the courage in *Three Guineas*. In the next part of this essay, my aim is to analyze carefully the aspects of Woolf's treatise which support my assumption that her account is about making-peace and not about war and patriarchal forms of keeping-peace.

The Question: Part II

The primary question Woolf addresses in *Three Guineas* is established in the following quotation:

> But, with the sound of the guns in your ears you have not asked us to dream. You have not asked us what peace is; you have asked us how to prevent war (259-260).

Paradigmatically, Woolf's courageous approach to the question is, I think, brilliant. Even today her response provides us with a constructive, theoretical and practical means for effecting peace. In the second part of this essay, I am not so much interested in messages intended by Woolf as I am in the way she constructs her response to the question of what women can do to prevent war.

Imaginatively, Woolf's response moves me through a series of other good questions which work well to demonstrate the utter futility of the question of how to prevent war in a patriarchal society. More impressively, by way of these questions Woolf encourages me to move beyond this futile question. In her opinion, once the clutter which this type of question creates is removed from the imagination, women and men will be freed to imagine a future without war. Simultaneously, the text offers a concrete way of assessing how I or others might put her theories into effect.

The Response and Constraints:

Before discussing Woolf's imagined future I want to speak about a response — not a solution — to the futile question of war. As I've mentioned, in her response to her own question, Woolf chooses to focus not on war but on the constraints and resources involved in making peace; these constraints place women outside the structures and professions (144) which generate and maintain warfare.

After demonstrating how women are excluded from all the major professions, she asks why any woman would want to take part in professional ceremonies which also systematically exclude them (114-115). She demonstrates, moreover, how dearly women pay for involvement in male-organized ceremonies and institutions which educate and support their brothers, fathers and husbands. Woolf reminds women that should they, in fact, decide to enter male institutions, they too will be supporting ongoing warfare and violence. This assumption is evident in the question, "how can we enter the professions and yet remain civilized human beings, human beings who discourage war . . ." (144)?

In raising the question of how male-organized institutions could affect women should they be allowed to participate, Woolf encourages readers to consider another question which often leads to heated debates amongst some feminists, especially those working in peace movements. This is the question of whether women are morally superior beings who naturally desire peace because of their reproductive and maternal roles which (supposedly) make them sexually distinct from males. In her discussion of how male-structured institutions co-opt both sexes, Woolf explicitly addresses this question, suggesting that women are no less capable of violence than men. Yet she is quick to point out,

> Scarcely a human being in the course of history has fallen to a woman's rifle; the vast majority of birds and beasts have been killed by you, not by us; and it is difficult to judge what we do not share (13-14).

In no way does Woolf assume that women are biologically better suited to making-peace than to making-war. However, it is clear from her work that unless institutions are changed and unless men change, women will continue to be disadvantaged by the structures which support and sustain war. For example, the following quote indicates Woolf's understanding of how women are disadvantaged in a patriarchal society,

> Therefore, if you insist upon fighting to protect me, or "our" country, let it be understood . . . that you are fighting a sex instinct which I cannot share; to procure benefits which I have not shared and probably will not share . . . (197).

The important point here, I think, is that while women do not share the benefits of a patriarchal society, like men we are nonetheless responsible, in Woolf's words, for the "tyrant" in ourselves that lets us believe in a repressive patriarchal system (163). In this manner, Woolf holds women and men equally accountable for their *"infantile fixations"* (255) which act through the practices of patriarchy to empower men and disempower women.

Woolf also holds women and men equally accountable for what she terms "adultery of the brain", crimes or sins committed for the sake of money (170). Again, Woolf quickly points out that for the most part, the option to commit "adultery of the brain" is primarily an option open to men because it is men who have access to economic resources far in excess of those available to most women, either in private or public realms (104-105). In view of this form of male power, are we then to assume that women are simply helpless in the face of these many constraints, with few resources? Woolf claims not, and demonstrates why.

The Future:
It is impossible to speak of Woolf's imagined future without reference to her understanding of formal education. Specifically, she asks her readers to imagine "What sort of education will teach the young to hate war" (42)? And secondly, she asks, "What kind of education should we bargain for" (42)? We can see that Woolf is calling for something quite different from the usual notion of education. For example, she writes about a "cheap college" which could meet very specific educational needs:

> It should explore the ways in which the mind and body can be made to cooperate; discover what new combinations make good wholes in human life. The teachers should be drawn from good "livers" as well as from good thinkers (62).

In her opinion, central to this kind of education is a holistic view of human beings and a concern for how such beings might organize without the hierarchical structures which divide and separate their minds and bodies, their thoughts and feelings. From this perspective, education would not be limited to educational institutions but would affect the everyday lives of real people. Within this vision of education, shared salaries and shared parenting might be considered the norm (214). For example, within Woolf's imagined "Society of Outsiders", there would be no hierarchies or leaders, and for this reason new ways of structuring society could emerge which would allow for easier cooperation amongst people (209). In the past decade we are, in fact, seeing the emergence of these types of institutions. In my own research area, for example, I have experienced the benefits of working in collectives structured quite differently from the traditional helping institutions which work to separate and divide and hence empower men and disempower women.

Resources:
Again in reference to her own question of how to prevent war, Woolf points readers to a newly-imagined future. This new direction encourages women to create new words and new methods and is referred to in the following quote,

> But as a result, the answer to your question must be that we can best help you to prevent war not by repeating your words and following your methods but by finding new words and creating new methods. We can best help you to prevent war not by joining your society but by remaining outside your society but in co-operation with its aim (260).

Woolf states that the best skill available to women to help develop a future in which peace is possible is the skill of absenting. To absent is to make-peace, as opposed to keeping-peace as women once knew it. And while Woolf does not actually use the term *making-peace* (this is my term) she does, I think, point out the advantages of absenting in relation to peace when she writes,

> To **absent** yourself — that is easier than to speak aloud at a bazaar, or to draw up rules of an original kind for playing games. Therefore it is worth watching very carefully to see what effect the experiment of absenting oneself has had — if any. The results are positive and they are encouraging (214).

In my analysis thus far, I have discussed how Woolf's text enables me to think differently about the issues of peace and how I regard this text as a treatise about peace, and not war. In my brief presentation of her theories, I demonstrate how her ideas concerning war focus on peace rather than on how to prevent war. My assumption about the differences between making-peace and keeping-peace is important. In principle, I argue that Woolf's notion of making-peace is akin to her notion of absenting. Further, I argue that many women are beginning to use absenting in a manner similar to that suggested by Woolf. In suggesting a link between the peace-making skills used in transition houses and the creative technique formulated by Woolf in response to her anguished concern with war, I attempt to show in my essay how women can similarly empower themselves through the practice of absenting from the violence of battering (and other war practices) for the explicit purpose of making, rather than keeping, peace.

In theory, absenting as a method of acquiring power is unique in that it requires neither hostile social practices nor attitudes of moral superiority as are common in the traditional male practices for keeping-peace. Making-peace techniques require only that women move from a passive position in times of violence and hostility to an active position through the practice of absenting. In this manner women will learn to absent themselves from male control and thereby free themselves to image healthier social practices which do not render them helpless. Always, of course, the problem that people face while waiting for others to change, whether in a global or a private sense, is the feeling of helplessness which can result from waiting for change to occur. Woolf's brilliant recourse is that of absenting to effect a kind of renewal and peace which one hopes will occur within the frame of adult accountability. When considering how women and men differently have, hold, and practise forms of power, it is important to consider the words of Holly Near who writes,

> I think by virtue of our very oppression we have been able to retain a kind of relationship to the life process that, had we been in a position of power over the last thousands and thousands of years, we might have lost (1984:252).

In the face of continuing oppression, it is important that women recognize and name, as Woolf does, our own strengths and weaknesses while analyzing those of the society in which we live. This is what I take to be important in my reading of *Three Guineas*. In my opinion, it is from this place which is our self, in conjunction with a critique of society, that we will begin to undo outmoded social practices and inventions.

For total disarmament to occur it is necessary that men assume primary accountability for the war practices they have created. Otherwise, women will be forced to withdraw their energy and support from the old systems and from the men who favour and support warfare and violence until they do accept accountability. If warfare is, as Margaret Mead (1949) suggests, an outmoded male invention (and I believe it is), it is certain that such an invention can be dismantled. Once dismantled, even at the ideological level, women's energy is freed. With this renewed energy women can create other skills with which to make-peace rather than continue wasting their energy in outmoded methods of keeping-peace. Thus absenting is a skill of prime importance to a world rapidly being destroyed by an invention — war — which long ago went out of fashion.

C: Glimmerings into the light

> I had been so humiliated in childhood, that my trust not only in others, but more essentially in myself, had been completely destroyed (Spring, 1987:116).

> For me, words were the beginning, the beginning of learning to see (Spring, 1987:102).

Dear Lily, Andrew and Virginia:

The abuse I experienced as a child is not something I thought consciously about until very recently. Therapists did not ask if I had been abused, and I did not volunteer the information. The question of why, for so long, I did not think it made a difference that I was a survivor of abuse is complex and one I am just beginning to address. Why, for example, does knowing suddenly make all the difference to me? How, I wonder, does the humiliation of abuse affect how I learn and know? How does it affect others? If abuse is as pervasive as is indicated in the work of Belenky et al. (1986), and if abuse negatively affects how students relate to figures of authority, how valuable then are mainstream educational practices which depend on authoritarian and hierarchical methods of instruction? How did abuse destroy my ability to trust myself, to trust others? Why when I wrote an essay about absenting practices, was I not conscious of how I had learned to split and absent myself when afraid? How did I learn to absent myself in my writing? Why did teachers working from feminist perspectives recognize that I absented myself in my writing? How do teachers reward students for removing themselves from their texts and producing 'objective' essays?

At the time of writing the Woolf essay I was unable to ask these kinds of questions. Since I had not then begun to write about my experiences of incest, abuse was simply not a factor in my existence. It became one only after I had written the stories introduced in Chapter 1. Each story, I am discovering, produces new and different questions. Once I began this process I went on to discover other ways to recover old memories. These memories are producing even more new questions.

My re-reading of the Woolf essay is one example of how I am using my own writing to recover old memories, for the purpose of asking new questions to better understand how I am affected by abuse. Until I wrote my *key* words "I am an incest survivor," I could not admit, to myself or to others, that my experience of abuse was real. Only through body symptoms did I feel my abuse as real and this, of course, was an unconscious experience. However, prior to admitting I was abused, I struggled in a variety of ways to make sense of the experience I had not yet named.

For example, I think I was drawn to the term *absent* because it was for me a key word. It describes my experience of "hiding in an essay". As well, it describes what happens to me when I am afraid. This kind of hiding has two forms. One, I retreat in a real sense: I remove myself from the situation. Two, I retreat in the sense of experiencing excess fear: I feel unable to breathe or to speak. When I first used the word in the Woolf essay, however, my sole interest was in how to use the term to describe my assumptions about battered women. I certainly did not think that the word was key to my experience. You may also have noticed in your reading of the Woolf essay that I highlighted the words *infantile fixations*. Again, I was not then conscious of how these words could be used to describe my (learned) infantile need to disappear when fearful. Rather, like Woolf, I was using the words to critique war practices as an infantile way of ordering society. I wonder if Woolf's interest in these terms was in any way connected to her abuse?

The words which I highlighted in the Woolf essay signalled something to me. Specifically, they signalled that aspects of my development were arrested: I could not write (anything) without experiencing fear and I did not know why. Had a teacher familiar with abuse literature or with the findings of educators like Ashton-Warner (1963) worked with me, with these words, at the time I wrote the essay, it is possible I could have begun earlier to identify the abuse which continued to harm me. This harm was active in that I felt badly about myself, my writing capability and my ability to teach. Nonetheless, because I was able to work as I did with the Woolf text, with a teacher who supported me, I was at least preparing myself, emotionally and intellectually, for an eventual confrontation with my memories of abuse.

Prior to the confrontation I was not conscious of how my behaviour was shaped by abuse, though at some level I had not forgotten it. Mostly I assumed it was not significant. Contradictorily, however, I knew that I could not speak about it. Thus, it was very important. At another level, I knew abuse as symptoms, though again I did not connect them with abuse. For the most part I assumed my symptoms were signs of my failures as a human being, the one in the family who seemed unable to get herself together. Thus it was for survival that I learned to live my splits. How could I be otherwise, given the conditions of the society in which I live?

Theoretically, had I not learned how to split myself, I probably would have committed suicide, or alternately succumbed to the madness which for many years I feared. Instead, I learned to survive and got on with it. In being forced to get on with it because of the conditions of this society, I allowed the status quo to move forward, unchallenged, and I lived in a state of tension and fear. As an individual, I learned to absorb the ugliness of a culture intent upon reproducing social harmony through illusion. Because I had not yet learned to critique the social practices which make abuse possible, I absorbed blame at the individual level. Similarly, I learned to see the problem solely in terms of another individual (my brother) rather than viewing it as a social problem which encased us both, however differently. This individualizing of the problem then worked to prevent me from examining the real problem: a male-organized society in which my brother was accorded power not available to me. Until I was taught to examine the social conditions which make abuse possible, I could neither resist it nor move beyond it. To learn this, however, demands more than an intellectual replaying of the trauma. In my case, I did not feel empowered until I wrote from an inner place where I could find the key words to name my experience. The Woolf (1938) essay marks one of the means by which I began the long process of learning to trust the knowledge and feelings provoked by her words.

No longer do I think it incidental that I began recovering myself in both a classroom context and in a larger institution where I felt safe (enough) to write the words which were key to exposing a previously untouched part of myself. That this process began while working with teachers (mostly women and a few men) for whom feminist perspectives are primary is also not incidental. Belenky et al. (1986) document how difficult it is for many women, abused and not abused, to learn with male teachers in authoritarian settings. They note, for example, that abused women often learn in new ways once they are able to change how they relate to authority figures (58). As their study indicates, this new learning is difficult because most teachers guiding women's learning are men (217), even though women now make up half the student population at the university level. Further complicating this situation is the fact that few teachers, whether female or male, have considered the theoretical implications of gender in an academic setting, particularly as it relates to women's learning, abuse, and relationship to authority. This is a problem in that many women, through male abuse and authority, are taught to doubt the validity of their achievements (60). That sexual abuse can prevent women from developing an inner self-authority is a problem not addressed in most theories of education.

Given that sexual abuse is pervasive and that there is a dearth of texts which analyze the relationship of abuse to gender and relations of power, theorists of education would do well to re-examine Woolf's (1938) theories of education. Educators must use their imaginations to create ways to open windows and doors for students suffering from any kind of trauma. I know that my own opening would not have happened had I not worked with teachers able to care both for themselves and for others. I know, too, I could not have moved to a safer place to begin the long process of re-learning to see myself through my own experience, and not through the reflection and experience of others, if I had not begun to work with educators who dared to critique the status quo. Only in such a learning environment could I reclaim my self-authority. This is not an easy task, but it is one I began to take up with teachers able to work with feminist perspectives. Recalling the words of Fraser, it is important to recognize, however, that not every abused woman will have the education, social resources, and the vast amount of personal support to "fight back" (1987:252).

Love and Solidarity.

> What a dangerous activity reading is; teaching is (Ashton-Warner, 1963:14).

I am humbled by the amount of power entrusted to me in the work of teaching. Using words, I am able to name and shape the world in ways which are not always apparent to me. I know, for example, that what I say and do is often received by my students in ways which I cannot possibly foresee. I know this because I recall that the words and actions of my teachers affected me in ways perhaps not apparent to them. Recognizing the power of words, I tread carefully with students. I claim the assumptions informing my work, while teaching them to claim their assumptions. The problem, of course, is to find methods for examining our respective assumptions, else they lie in waiting, shaping all that we say and do. Autobiography, I suggest, is one such way.

In Chapter 6, I will examine further how I am learning to examine my own assumptions, in particular that knowledge is socially constructed and therefore capable of being changed.

chapter six

A: Contradictions and a Desire for Harmony

Our perceived need for harmony is particularly detrimental to the expansion of our knowledge. Like wishful thinking, the need for harmony ornaments ugly inconsistencies, plasters over the cracks (Haug et al., 1987:69).

I'm concerned with a practical problem: how do you get students . . . to understand the concept of ideology? Because without it, I really think one can teach nothing worthwhile at all, unless you want them to learn like parrots (Williamson, 1981/82:81).

One method of story analysis proved in our experience to be fruitful, namely the tracing of contradictions (Haug et al., 1987:68).

*I find it difficult to recall if I ever lived any part of my life without desiring harmony. I think my need for harmony is related to a deep need to **appear normal**. At a very early age I learned to value appearing normal: I had to cover(up) (appear outwardly orderly and tidy) the fact that I had been abused. Over time I learned to attract deliberate attention to my **dress**. Unconsciously, I wanted people to know an external me. Outside was safe. My secret was safe. Internal harmony depended upon this safety. Thus, harmonious feelings were key to my survival. Like many women, I learned to appease and to keep peace. I needed calm. My need for internal calmness was so intense that, for example, for years I was unable* to listen to classical music. Music produced feeling and it produced chaos. Feeling and chaos is frightening when the need for harmony is paramount. Not knowing why I required inner harmony, I learned to live(out) one of many illusions and in so doing I helped to reproduce, amongst other beliefs, the idea that I was somehow at fault for my own abuse.

It has been difficult for me to grasp **ideology** as a concept and knowledge therefore as **socially constructed** because I learned so deeply to live in the realm of illusion. Unable to examine the illusions which organized my experience, I learned to pretend. Unable to examine the ideas which organized my pretence, I learned to parrot the illusions which organized me. This orientation is, of course, rewarded in an educational system based on rote methods of learning. However, I did not necessarily benefit from my ability to learn by rote because abuse had also taught me to be suspicious of the status quo, including rote learning.

The rote method is antithetical to learning how to question. As a victim, I found it difficult to question because I needed to protect the illusion that I had not been abused. In a similar manner, I learned to accept other kinds of illusions such as the illusion that I live in a free and democratic society. It is very difficult for any person — and perhaps more so for a person bound by trauma — to question the assumptions which organize social principles and ideologies; that is, unless we are taught to critique them. Without learning how to critique we learn like parrots.

In Chapter 5, I introduced an essay written prior to my decision to speak openly about abuse. When I wrote it, I was neither conscious of, nor able to grapple with, the abuse which shaped my social history. I had not yet learned how to do this. Using autobiographical memory work and focusing on the context in which the essay was written, I began to examine how I had learned to produce and reproduce illusions. At the time of writing essay one, I was not yet working from an inner self-authority. Rather, I borrowed from the inner authorities of others; in the case of essay one, the authority was Virginia Woolf.

In Chapter 6, I will focus on a second essay which I wrote as a graduate student, again prior to my decision to write about abuse. My aim here is to explicate, from a focus on this essay, how I began (intellectually) to understand ideology as a concept and knowledge as socially organized. I think the writing of this essay enabled me to understand intellectually that illusions and ideologies are created and reproduced by people. I was not able, however, to apply this knowledge directly to my own experience. In other words, while I began to understand in principle that ideology is a concept, I could not relate this knowledge to myself. Rather, I was able only to relate it to my understanding of others, such as battered women. In this manner my learning was intellectual. When later I began *to apply this knowledge to an internalized way of knowing, I began to shift from (what I now consider) a limited intellectual perspective. I will speak more specifically about this transfer in Chapter 7.*

Together we made the volcano erupt, I, through writing, talking, realizing, she through surrounding me with the complete reassurance that it was safe to do so, that she was not afraid of my anger . . . (Spring, 1987:108).

Dear Lily, Andrew and Virginia:

I am sitting at my word processor and wondering, as I look out from an upstairs window, about the changes I am experiencing. I feel happy as I recognize change in myself. In part, this is connected to my newly-discovered love of teaching. And it is connected to the fact that there is something about teaching which enables me to change. In my work with students I feel less anxious about looking for right answers. Instead, I delight in asking new kinds of questions. Similarly, I am teaching students the value of asking questions. I am discovering that students can readily understand ideology as a concept if they are taught to examine first the assumptions which organize their own experiences. This process is exciting, in part because these new questions are informing my writing and, in part because it enables me to move away from a dualistic (either/or) approach to learning and knowing (an approach I learned early through my desire to achieve harmony) to perspectives which enable me to understand ideology as a concept and knowledge, therefore, as socially constructed.

In my letter of today I will attempt to explain how the writing of this second essay further prepared me for my decision to write about abuse. Without having written about abuse I could not, of course, write from my own perspective: I was, you recall, locked into the perspective of the other, the abuser, as well as the male-organized ideologies which make abuse possible and which prevent women from telling. Essay two is important because it was my first attempt to come to terms intellectually, in writing, with the notion of ideology as a concept. I view this shift as crucial because without an understanding of ideology I was unable to move beyond the debilitating effects of abuse to a perspective with which to critique abusive practices. Without such a critique I could only reproduce my silence. In re-reading of this account, I realize that I produced in this essay a rather one-dimensional, harmonious picture of how I learn and know.

In other words, I wrote as if the learning described in the essay happened merely by producing the text when, in fact, other events working in conjunction with the preparation of the essay precipitated the learning. I point this out because I think, as do Belenky et al. (1986), that much of women's learning does occur outside the classroom, in part because so much of what we are expected to learn is not relevant to our experiences as women. What I learned in the production of essay two was influenced by other events, which I will discuss later in this letter. A recognition of the complexity of any learning process is vital to producing educational theory, else researchers will produce inaccurate theories of how women or men learn. How then do I remember the learning which resulted in writing this second essay?

The first time I wrote about my experience of the class for which I produced this second essay was in the second or third construction of my PhD thesis proposal. It reads as follows:

> *Something important happened to me this year in a class concerned with the social organization of knowledge. By way of an intellectual botanizing exercise, the professor requested that I learn to ride a metaphorical bike. From this exercise and through questioning, active reading, writing, and description, I began to see how knowledge is organized by social practices which can render invisible ideological boundaries. From this botanizing exercise, designed to ferret out ideological practices, both mine and others, I began to see that I'd written about an aspect of the battered women's movement as though I knew the truth of the situation. Through a series of tricks, I'd written in such a way as to obscure my ideological claims (Smith, 1974a:45). I think this method of writing is a problem, in that all counter ways of describing the situation are then measured against what I believe to be the truth. In analyzing this process at work in my own writing, I am better able to understand what it means to speak of socially-produced knowledge. Thus, knowing myself as a producer of knowledge enables me to move from a concern with producing and reproducing the truth, to an interest in asking better questions, with less interest in seeking right answers (Brookes, 1986:4-5).*

Something important did happen to me in this class taught by a dedicated and committed feminist. The teacher required me to learn in ways I had not before learned, primarily as a result of the botanizing exercise. This exercise, as I understood it, was intended to teach students how knowledge is socially organized. I understood the exercise to be a specialized reading practice. The professor had devised a rather unique method for teaching students to consciously read critically. In other words, she did not regard reading as a non-political exercise which students naturally knew how to do. Rather, she assumed students could learn, with practice, how to read effectively the conditions of their everyday world. In my opinion, unique to her assumption (which I support) is the idea that graduate students need further reading instruction.

Students were expected to choose a text of interest to themselves. The intent of the exercise was to learn to read critically in order to understand the assumptions and ideologies which organize a text. Students were encouraged to develop a question of interest to themselves based on their reading of the text. This question would then become the focus of a re-reading of the text, after which students were to write a critique based on their questions. To address their questions, students were expected to use detail, description, analysis, and further questioning. When this first stage of the exercise was completed, the professor would respond in writing to the student's work.

The second stage of the botanizing exercise involved further readings and new questions which would, in turn, inform the writing of a final critique (it is this final critique which I include in this chapter). As I understood, botanizing was a means for teaching students to observe in a thorough and careful manner, as would be expected in any botany experiment. The professor's aim was to teach students to see beneath the obvious, to see how the data of the chosen text was organized to present an ideological perspective. Key to this was simultaneously knowing the perspectives and assumptions each student took to her or his reading of a text and knowing how to deconstruct the assumptions and perspectives with which the author organized the text. This way of knowing began yet another phase of my preparedness to ask questions about my experiences of abuse:

> So, as we stand at the moment in history when we still have choice... it is of the very greatest importance which questions we ask, because by the questions we ask we set the answers that we will arrive at, and define the paths along which future generations will be able to advance (Mead, 1949:13).

Learning about ideology and knowledge as socially constructed was not, as I suggest above, a one-time, one-dimensional happening or recognition. In other words, I did not learn about ideology and knowledge as socially constructed and then, in a linear manner, use this knowledge to analyze my experience. Essay two is, however, an important 'marker' for me; it marks a time of personal transformation as I was learning to think differently about my world. In your reading of this essay I ask that you imagine the larger context in which I wrote. It was, I suggest, a combination of events and a series of crises, and not the writing of one essay only, which prepared me for the eventual confrontation with the abuses which silently organized me.

While I was writing and thinking about the ideas I present in this essay, I was also involved in another graduate class. There was, for me, an intimate and vital connection between the work of these two courses. Hindsight suggests that I began to conceptualize ideology precisely because of events occurring in these courses and other events, which marked my time outside the classroom. Nonetheless, the work of essay two is in my memory the basis for a pivotal learning experience.

I am concerned that I initially assumed I had learned to examine ideology as a result of the work I produced for one course. As a teacher I am aware that learning shifts are seldom related to one event. To assume otherwise does not take into account the multiplicity of factors which shape how most people learn. One-dimensional assumptions about learning are not, however, uncommon. It is, for example, a one-dimensional way of learning and presenting which is rewarded and encouraged in most schooling practices. How often, for example, are students rewarded or encouraged to rewrite and rework old papers? In fact, an important aspect of the botanizing exercise is the writing and re-writing of our perspectives. This same teacher worked hard to accommodate and appreciate that which students did not yet understand.

As a student and teacher re-reading essay two, I am both frightened by the rigidity of my writing and excited by the learning for which it stands. It is, however, from this point of resistance that I will begin to reconstruct and remember the missing aspects of those texts which are key to how I came to know ideology and hence knowledge as socially organized. Thus Chapter 6 is an analysis of how I think I began to learn, at a deep bodily level, to interact differently with authority figures and texts as authorities, and in so doing to know better my own self-authority. In other words, my aim is to critique how I think I was preparing to refuse the illusions which had for so long separated my mind and my body.

Love and Solidarity.

B: Re-considering the Binding and Unbinding of Ideological Practices

Binding and Unbinding Ideological Practices

<Essay Two>

Introduction

In this essay I will describe how I learned about ideology as a social practice which informs, often unconsciously, the texts which I and others produce. My intent is to discuss how I learned about ideological practices in a university course designed to encourage students to think about the social organization of knowledge. Specifically, I will discuss how a class project ostensibly designed to ferret out ideological practices helped me understand knowledge as socially organized.

Based on my reading of the work of Smith, I will discuss the relationship of ideology to knowledge as a methodological point of departure within textual studies, in an attempt to "assert a difference between ideology and social science as a critical procedure" (1974:41). The data base for my study is: a) a news story about battered women; b) my response to this story (the botanizing exercise); and c) the professor's response to the botanizing exercise. My intent is to examine, from my understanding of what it means to botanize a text, how the third document was the catalyst for my better understanding of the methodological difference between ideology and sociology as a critical procedure; in other words, I understood that knowledge is socially organized to present certain ideologies and perspectives.

In my opinion, the purpose of the botanizing exercise is to teach students to recognize ideologies at work in texts, both their own and those of authors whom students attempt to critique. The botanizing exercise teaches students to do more than simply deconstruct arguments. It is intended to teach students how to see beneath the constructions of any text to understand how ideologies are organized around particular perspectives. To do this is to understand knowledge as socially organized.

The following is a reconstruction of how I learned to botanize texts. Given that the method of botanizing was not outlined in written form, I do not assume that my understanding of the exercise is shared by the professor concerned. As I recall, the professor requested that each student choose a text of interest to her or him. The exercise was to read carefully a selected text and a) develop a question of the text of interest to students; b) use this question to critique the assumptions and ideologies which shape the text; c) examine the assumptions which students as readers bring to their analysis of texts. Ostensibly, the purpose of the exercise was to teach students to see ideology at work in texts. Once viewed in this manner, students understand better the concept of knowledge as socially organized.

The process through which this learning was expected to occur also involved three steps. Each step was predicated on the assumption that students would describe in detail what they observed when reading their chosen text. In step one students were required to select a text to which they would respond in writing. In step two the professor was required to respond to the students' written responses. Following this, step three involved using the two responses — the professor's and the student's — to organize a further analysis of the selected text.

For my botanizing exercise, I chose to examine a newspaper story about a shelter shortage. I chose it because I thought the newspaper reporter was presenting the data inaccurately. This assumption came from my experience of working closely with the shelter movement. The professor's response to my first attempt to botanize my text indicated that I had not learned to do so. My struggle to respond to her comments informed my learning in another way. An explication of this other way forms the work of this essay.

I think I experienced a shift in how I learn and know as a result of the exercise. This happened as I worked to make sense of the professor's response to my first attempt to botanize a text. More specifically, when the professor responded to my first analysis with the comment that she felt something (she did not identify what) was missing in my analysis, I became obsessed with the implications of her comment.

The Problematic

In her response to my initial attempts, the professor begins by stating that she thinks there is a problem in my work. She notes that even though I make reference in one or two places to an "actual reality," which I claim to know, I do not indicate what this reality is. Without this "missing something" she has difficulty holding on to the "alternative method" of reading suggested by my account. Without this information, she asserts, it is difficult for her, as reader, to do a 'proper' (proper is used here to denote a critical reading of a given text) re-reading of the news story I attempt to analyze.

The significance of the professor's comments was not immediately apparent to me. I did not know what she meant when she said something was missing in my critique of the news story, nor did I know what a proper re-reading of this story would entail. I assumed, however, that I knew what was missing in my reading of the reporter's account I was attempting to botanize. And while I was by implication calling for an alternative reading — a correct version to replace his incorrect version of the actual reality — I did not in the early stages of my work explicitly grasp the broader methodological and theoretical implications of my request. In fact, the professor's comments did not present themselves as a problematic for me until I reread Smith's work. Only from this rereading was I able to see how my either/or stance (either the reporter is correct or I am correct) had created an ideological boundary that prevented me from doing critical sociology. Hence I reached an understanding of the professor's comments about the *something missing* from my botanizing necessary for a proper re-reading of the news story.

The Ideological Practice of Sociology

My initial reaction to the professor's comments about my first attempts to botanize was to assume that I had, in fact, missed something reading the text. Thus, to do a *proper* re-reading of the news story I needed only to return to the text to gather support for my rather indignant assertion that the reporter had written inaccurately about an aspect of the shelter movement. Importantly, I assumed his perspective to be incorrect because I had information, based on my work in shelters, which proved him wrong. The questions and solutions to the problem described in his newspaper report did not directly address what I perceived to be the *'real' reality* of the situation. In other words, his assumptions about a refuge shortage, as analyzed in his news story, did not mesh with my assumptions about how to remedy the shortage.

What I could not grasp in the early stages of the botanizing exercise was the concrete way in which both I and the reporter were bound to our respective, constructed versions of *actual reality,* which in turn were bound to our differing ideological practices: his to the ideological practices of the institution of the *Globe and Mail,* and mine to the ideological practices of the institution of the battered women's shelter movement. Without an understanding of how closely we were bound to the practices of the respective institutions which shaped and informed our perspectives about shelter work (that this was, in fact, the *actual reality* I sought to understand, but could not yet articulate), I was unable to consider the possibility that a *proper* re-reading did not entail simply *getting the facts* right. The idea that our attachment to differing ideological practices, unelucidated by either of us, would tell me more about the *actual reality* of the situation that would *right facts* was not yet a serious consideration.

Confused, attempting to understand what the professor meant by a *proper* re-reading of the news story, I took all my beliefs about the *actual reality* of the situation, with all the professor's comments in tow, to a re-reading of Smith's work. My aim was to find a better method of re-reading the story of my choice. This is what I discovered.

In her article "The Ideological Practice of Sociology", Smith argues that "ideology as contrasted with knowledge identifies rather the interested procedures which people use as a means not to know" (1974:40). She states further her view that social scientists have "worked within the ideological boundary without realizing it was there" (41). This *way* of working within ideological boundaries is, according to Smith, a way of thinking which is both "distinctive and describable" (41). She writes:

> To think ideologically is therefore to think in a distinctive and describable way. Ideas and concepts, as such, are not ideological. They are ideological by virtue of being constituted and used in ideological ways (41).

In recognizing that ideology is a practice or method of constructing knowledge about "actualities of what living people do" (44), it becomes a logical step to study ideology within the actual practices of social relations as they occur in living or textual modes. Without such a grounding Smith is, I think, correct to assume that theories or concepts ruptured from practice and the practical relations and activities of people (45) are a mere "substitute for reality" (45).

Motivated by my need to do a *proper* re-reading of the news story, I set out to understand how academics are able to separate theories about people's practices from their actual practices. It was, then, a relief to discover within Smith's work an explanation for why I did not know about the boundaries keeping me from a *proper* reading of the news story. It was a greater relief to discover (I was not innately closed, and perhaps not forever destined to move in ideological circles) Smith's analysis (1974a) of three methodological tricks (45) — the original from *The German Ideology* (in Smith, 1974a) — which work continuously to (unconsciously) bind researchers to ideological practices. These tricks are as follow:

Trick One:

> Separate what people say they think from the actual circumstances in which it is said, from the actual empirical conditions of their lives and from the actual individuals who said it.

Trick Two:

> Having detached the ideas, arrange them to demon-

strate an order among them which accounts for what is observed (Marx and Engels describe this as making "mystical connections . . .").

Trick Three:

> Then change the ideas into a *person*, that is they are constituted as distinct entities (e.g. value, pattern, norm, belief system, etc.) to which agency (or possible causal efficacy) may be attributed. And re-attribute them to *reality* by attributing them to actors who now represent the ideas (Smith, 1974a:45-46).

What is particularly problematic about the use of these tricks in ideological practices is that, "In our kind of society ideological practice is not remediable by critique alone" (Smith, 1974a:54). For this reason, writes Smith:

> Examination of the relation between the ideological uses of the forms of thought and the actualities of living individuals is subject to that very rule which Marx recommends, namely to think of this relation not merely in the conceptual or theoretical mode, but as an enterprise in discovering how it is mediated in the practical activities of men (sic). A shift in the direction of attention is not enough to disclose the lineaments in actuality of the *profound philosophical problem* and resolve it. This critique is rather a problem for investigation, for discovery, a Sociological work in itself. It is this work I want to recommend (Smith, 1974a:54).

To know this, however, is not necessarily to do it.

Approach

In contrast with Volosinov (1973), Vygotsky (1962) and other supporters of Karl Marx, I think Smith is revolutionary in her ability to locate theory in practice. While not specifically concerned with language and development, she nonetheless demonstrates practically a *way* of approaching social problems. Methodologically, Smith locates problems in their particular social and historical contexts for the purpose of preventing the privileged from uncritically assuming relations between observable data (1974:48). Central to Smith's work is her ability to actualize concepts, such as language, within practice, rather than creating elaborate theoretical explanations which remain ungrounded in the practice (speech acts) to which it refers, thereby creating yet another *ideological practice*. Smith's useful working rule for avoiding construction of ideological practices is "to insist upon passing through the *forms of thought* to a description of what people do to make that concept or that statement something that can be said" (1974:47). In this manner (theory) language is grounded in practice.

Technique

Description is central to Smith's methodological approach to an analysis of a problem. Like Vygotsky, Freire, and Ortega y Gasset and others, Smith's methodological approach is important in that it examines social practices and problems from the perspective people's everyday experience. In this sense, Smith's development of the botanizing exercises is a concrete way of allowing students to confront methodological problems in their own research.

In teaching researchers how to confront social problematics, Smith insists that they describe the many and varied mandated courses of action which affect how subjects confront the problems which institutions present to their everyday lives. In this manner, the ideological procedures and practices of the ruling apparatus become descriptively and analytically observable in the *actual reality* of people's experiences. In researching these experiences, Smith (1974a) emphatically insists "upon the practice of formulating a description of how it is done and by whom as a first and elementary rule of sociological enquiry" (1974:48).

The use of description as an analytical tool is fundamental to Smith's methodological approach. In her article, "Women's Perspective as a Radical Critique of Sociology" (1974b), she acknowledges and theorizes the researcher's presence in any research project. Smith talks specifically about the work of Jean Briggs and her ethnographic study of how Eskimo [Inuit] people "structure and express emotion" (Smith, 1974b:11), suggesting that according to Briggs, "the tensions and quarrels were the living texture in which she learnt what she describes" (11). It is obviously important to Smith that Briggs' knowledge developed "in the context of those relationships" (11). Key here is the acknowledgment of a direct relationship between theory and practice.

One of the more obvious ways in which Smith inserts herself as researcher into the processes underlying her research projects is through development of continually evolving techniques for working with other researchers on joint projects. These techniques are structured to study people in the context of institutional reality; they include ongoing development of questions (participant observation) as they emerge in the context of a particular project. Within this ethnomethodology Smith (1975) is sensitive to "different experiences of the world and different bases of experience" (11) so as not to impose, and rather to acknowledge the researcher's effect upon the research. Central to what Smith (1983) refers to as "The Ethnomethodology Discovery" is the view that:

> sense, rationality, facticity, etc. are essentially products of, and accomplished in, local historical settings. This has opened the way to the investigation of reasoning, facticity, rationality, sense-making not as processes going on in people's heads but as social practices (1983:2).

Early in my acquaintance with Smith's work, I found it difficult to imagine how researchers might insert themselves in their texts. I now think this difficulty is related to my earlier inability to grasp the importance of not being bound as researcher to ideology. I was frustrated by practices which failed to recognize theoretical analysis itself as actual social practice. Through an in-depth reading of Smith's work, in conjunction with the botanizing exercise, I began to understand better the effects of ideology in my work and thereby to see how I had previously been bound by ideologies which I had not learned to critique. Thus, through a more active reading of texts, I learned to approach them so as not to begin from the "assumption of the inertia of the text" (Smith, 1982:1).

As a result of learning how to read texts differently, I came to appreciate Smith's discussion of the active text as something that "might be thought of as more like a crystal which bends the light as it passes through" (1982:2) rather than as something inert (1). Ultimately however, Smith's approach enables readers to discover the ideological practices which bind, or blind, researchers to a documentary method of interpretation, thus preventing them from seeing the relationship of human practice to institutionalized and mandated courses of action. What Smith aims to do is prevent the construction of a *knowledge* which is ideological in the sense that it,

> preserves conceptions and means of description which represent the world as it is for those who rule it, rather than as it is for those who are ruled (1985:267).

Thus, central to Smith's work is the concept of a social organization of knowledge which will direct "us to attend to both the terms of the relation and how that relation is socially organized" (1975:257). These relations, Smith argues, may be examined in an *active* reading of any text. Central to such a reading is knowledge of how ideological practices operate to preserve mandated courses of action. To *observe* without this knowledge is to observe in the realm of abstraction apart from the *actual reality* of an unstated or *missing* framework. Hence, as in my critique of the news story, *something* (that which binds me to ideological practices) remains unstated (or understated), and doesn't allow for a *proper* re-reading of the news story. By this I understand Smith to mean a reading which allows or enables readers to see how texts are socially constructed to present ideology in particular ways; to know this is to read properly in Smith's terms.

The Texts
It would be a meaningless exercise to describe how I learned about the construction of ideological practices without a discussion of the texts which aided my change in thinking about critical sociology. In this section, I will include the following texts: a news story about battered women, my response to the news story (the botanizing exercise), and the professor's response to the botanizing exercise.

The model I use to present these texts as ethnographic data is adopted from Smith's paper, "The Active Text: A textual analysis of the social relations of public textual discourse" (1982). This paper significantly aided me in altering my research approach. Specifically, I drew from her description and analysis of texts as public discourse, in working through how the three tricks operated in the documentary method of interpretation.

In following Smith's description and analysis of two specific documents I saw the futility of "focusing upon the problems of two versions of the same event . . ." (1982:6). Instead, I began to appreciate the need for "addressing the problem of how they (the texts) were actively at work in the context of the social relations in which they arose" (1982:6). The technique Smith uses and which I adopt is to quote the texts verbatim, using a lettering and numbering of lines "to facilitate comparison and cross-reference . . ."

Part A below is quoted directly from the news story I selected as the text for my botanizing exercise. Part B is my response to this news story, which I aim to read in the proper manner taught by Dorothy Smith. In other words, this is my attempt to see ideology being constructed. Her response in Part C indicates that I did not do a proper reading. Frustrated, I wrote this essay to see if I could better understand the botanizing exercise. Her response to my essay, not included in Chapter 6, shows that I was finally able to understand the exercise. In fact, the exercise as a whole was instrumental to my understanding of knowledge as socially constructed.

PART A News Story:
Battered Women being turned away in refuge shortage

The Globe and Mail - Sean Fine

1 Nearly 70 women and children were turned away every week last
2 year from emergency shelters for battered women in Etobicoke
3 and community workers say the shortage has become even more
4 acute in the past month.
5 And in November, the Ontario Government will launch a
6 $220,000 Metro Toronto hotline for battered women and a
7 $400,000 television advertising campaign telling battered
8 women to seek help.
9 The women are "going to call and we'll say, "Gee, I wish
10 we could help you but we're all full,""'said Cheryl Gorman,
11 a staff worker at Interval House in Toronto, which turns
12 away more than nine women for every one accepted.
13 More women are seeking help not because more are being
14 beaten but probably because the issue's high public profile
15 has helped them to overcome their feelings of shame and
16 guilt, said Sue Eason of Ernestine's shelter for battered
17 women in Etobicoke.

Victims not turned away without help

18 The 22-bed shelter, which opened in August/1983 turned away
19 889 women and children last year. Etobicoke's other
20 shelter, the 7-year-old, 25-bed Women's Habitat, had to
21 turn away 2,426 people.
22 In Scarborough, the 28-bed Emily Stowe shelter for battered
23 women turns away about 10 people for every one accepted, as
24 does the North York Women's Shelter, spokesmen for both
25 shelters said.
26 These women are not simply turned away without help, said
27 Lois Heitner of Women's Habitat. Workers may ask for aid from
28 Metro Toronto's seven other privately run shelters, each of
29 which has between 20 and 30 beds, or from a handful of
30 hostels or the publicly run, 90-bed Peggy Ann Walpole House
31 in Toronto.

In Metro Toronto, there are about 340 beds for battered women. Two more planned shelters still are several months from opening, said John Jagt, spokesman for Metro Toronto's hostel operations.

Ms Heitner and other workers worry that some women are staying in abusive relationships partly because of the difficulty of finding a shelter.

Those who cannot wait may wind up in hotels where rents are paid by Metro or Peel Social Services, or at a full Walpole House, Ms Heitner said.

"More and more often, we are forced to tell women that they will have to sleep on (the Walpole) floor and "try again tomorrow" said Interval House's Kerri Kwinter. "We are naturally concerned about women who, given this last option, choose to remain in violent situations."

A spokesman for Walpole House denied that families are sleeping on the floor, saying that when it gets crowded, cots are supplied.

Shelters can mean a new life for some women and their children, workers said. Counselling, peer support and applications for welfare and subsidized housing provide a start.

"No woman makes it to a shelter without tremendous strength," Ms Heitner said. Some, however, make it no further because of the housing shortage.

The housing crisis is one of the major factors inducing women to return home," said Lynda Morton, an anthropology graduate from the University of Toronto who studied post-shelter housing for Ernestine's shelter.

Lack of affordable housing and discrimination by landlords against single mothers are also causing women to stay longer in shelters. Some women are staying for several months, though six weeks to two months is the preferred maximum.

According to a Canada Mortgage and Housing Corp. survey, Etobicoke has an apartment vacancy rate of 0.3 per cent. That leaves only 133 vacancies in the municipality's 44,348 apartments.

Even that number is deceptively high for many single parents since it does not take into account overpriced adult-only or poorly maintained apartments, Ms Morton said. Etobicoke has the highest proportion of adult-only

74 apartment buildings in Metro Toronto, Ms Heitner said.
75 One 35-year-old Missisauga woman, who has lived at
76 Ernestine's for the past two months, said after a 1983 stay
77 at a shelter she returned to a husband who had been beating
78 her for six years, partly because she could not find a place
79 to live.
80 "I was afraid to go to bed at night because I didn't know
81 what kind of mood he'd be in. I'd pretend to be asleep."
82 She stayed with her husband so long because "I believed I
83 deserved the treatment. I kept on thinking maybe I did
84 something.

PART B Botanizing Exercise
Anne-Louise Brookes

The following is my written analysis of the above newspaper article. This is my first attempt to "botanize" a text of interest to me:

85 Reading as a feminist and researcher interested in the social
86 and political concerns of transition house workers, and
87 battered women for, and with whom they work, my attention was
88 drawn to a recent Globe and Mail news item. This item
89 caught my attention because its bold headline gave voice
90 to a concern that battered women are "being turned away in
91 refuge shortage". Knowing it to be a fact that the number
92 of women seeking help from transition houses exceeds the
93 number of available houses, I was pleased to see the
94 expressed interest of the Globe and Mail.
95 A second and third reading of this item curtailed my
96 pleasure. In a curious manner, Sean Fine, the reporter of
97 this item
98 manages to pose questions and answers to the
99 problem of a refuge shortage in such a way as to obscure
100 the actual reality of this shortage. In so doing, he shifts
101 our attention from the particular problem to a more
102 abstract, general concern with "housing shortages" for
103 which it becomes difficult to imagine a solution. My intent
104 in the following exercise is to analyze some of the
105 practices used by Fine to produce a text quite different from
106 his stated concern.
107 Fine's method of collecting and arranging information is

immediately apparent. To better appreciate how Fine has arranged his factual account by presenting facts which implicitly correspond to questions made invisible by the method of presentation, I will in this exercise discuss his twenty paragraph news items as five separate units, which, but for a small disjuncture between unit one and two, are linked to one another.

Having alerted the reader to a refuge shortage Fine, in unit one, provides the reader with facts about the actual numbers of battered women being turned away from "emergency shelters" in Etobicoke. A discussion of this shortage is immediately obscured, however, by the presentation of two facts: one, a recent government decision to set up a $220,000 Metro Toronto hotline for battered women and two, the implementation of a $4000,000 television advertising campaign *telling* battered women to seek help.

The question of why this government decision was made, in view of the fact that the number of available shelters does not currently meet the demand, is obscured in a number of ways. First, the reader is alerted to the fact that the government is *at least* doing something to aid battered women. That this highlighted fact does not correspond with the actual reality of there being a shortage is again obscured by the practice of not directly addressing the contradiction. Rather, in response to Fine's implied questioning of the decision, Cheryl Gorman, a worker at Interval House, is quoted as saying, "Gee, I wish we could help you but we're all full". Gorman's response has the effect of shifting our attention from further questioning about the non-so-obvious discrepancy between government action and the reality of a refuge shortage to a more immediate concern with Gorman's implied and "un-professional" use of the vernacular to address a serious issue. This shift of concern draws the reader's attention away from the real problem at hand: a refuge shortage. In this way the reader may lose interest in the problem.

In unit two Fine assures the reader that victims are "not turned away without help". Help is indeed available, and the fact that "10 people for every one accepted" are turned away is unproblematic because workers will "ask for aid from Metro

149 Toronto's seven other privately run shelters". Obscuring
150 the fact that these shelters too cannot accommodate battered
151 women, Fine reports that the workers may turn to a handful
152 of hostels, or the *publicly-run* 90-bed Peggy Ann Walpole
153 House in Toronto. In all, Fine reproduces facts to show
154 that 340 beds for battered women are available
155 in Metro, with two more shelters in planning.
156 Not stressed by Fine is that children and non-battered
157 women in distress will also occupy these 340 beds. Equally
158 unstated is a discussion of the differences between
159 privately funded and publicly funded shelters. This
160 difference is essential to an understanding of the
161 political aims of transition houses which do more than
162 simply *refuge* women.
163 Fine, in unit three, alludes to the workers who express
164 concern about women who return to abusive
165 relationships because of difficulties in finding adequate
166 shelter. Not discussed is the issue of what constitutes
167 adequate shelter.
168 This issue is glossed over in Fine's reporting
169 of the fact that in the case of refusal
170 other resources are available. It is possible for women
171 to stay in hotels, with rent paid by Metro or Peel
172 social services. Alternately, women may find a cot
173 (or possibly the floor) to rest on at Walpole House. Again,
174 hidden in this discussion is the fact that such services
175 are available on a short-term basis (one or two nights),
176 which contrasts the longer stay at transition houses,
177 where peer support is available; this is not possible
178 in short-term hostels. Again, the reader is encouraged
179 not to worry about the *few* who really could secure aid
180 if they truly needed it.
181 In unit four we are led to view an even graver problem:
182 the problem of post-shelter housing on which Fine reports
183 at length. But again, we are encouraged not to worry
184 because it is a problem which the professionals (Lynda
185 Morton) are investigating. In this unit, we are indirectly
186 reminded that many people, not merely battered women, are
187 facing a serious housing crisis.
188 Finally, having moved the reader in unit four to a more
189 abstract concern with a general housing shortage for
190 which no solution is apparent, Fine in unit five leads

191 us to believe that the refuge shortage is not the real
192 issue. Moreover, through his curious practice of
193 producing facts which have little to do with a refuge
194 shortage, we as readers are then separated from the actual
195 reality of this shortage, thus the ideological circle is
196 complete (within which these facts may be reproduced).
197 Quite apart from the actual problem of a refuge shortage,
198 Fine encourages us (by describing an
199 individual woman who has been battered) to imagine that
200 battered women can instigate change quite apart from the shelter
201 movement.
202 Thus, through a process clearly not intended, Fine acts
203 in the interest of a government bent on preserving a
204 capitalist system. He has produced a text which will per-
205 petuate the myth of individualism.
206 Basically, this text stands opposed to the aims and
207 goals of women who work within the movement to aid battered
208 women through social and political
209 change.

Lastly, I suggest that Fine's refusal to seriously consider the aims of the movement is apparent in his use of the term *refuge*; this is a term seldom used by women in the shelter movement.

PART C *Professor's Comments on my botanizing exercise*

210 This is very interesting — but there's a problem. It is
211 less in the analysis than in the reader's competence.
212 You refer at one or two places to the *actual reality* etc.
213 But a reader like myself, like presumably most readers of
214 such a news item, can only read (only knows how to read)
215 the surface of the text. What is missing in your account
216 of what that reality is, what is it that you and the North
217 York worker know about that reality as the alternative
218 method of reading which you and she are able to do? I find
219 it actually hard, in reading your account, to hold in place
220 the alternative method of reading which you are suggesting.
221 Something is missing that makes it difficult for the reader of your
222 botanizing exercise to do a *proper* re-reading of the news story.

Due to time and space constraints, I will not reconstruct Smith's analysis of the two texts used for her *Active Text* paper though I, in fact, use much of this analysis to approach my data base — the three texts — of this paper. My remarks about the three texts are general except to note that in different ways all three accounts, like those in Smith's analysis, lift a specific local event into "public textual discourse" (1982:17). Of this kind of process, Smith writes:

> Through we cannot trace the social production of these accounts independently of what they themselves have to tell us about it, each displays the social organization of its grounding in an actuality. Again I would remind the reader that what we are addressing is the events as worked up in accounts of them and never the events themselves (1982:17).

Discussion

Texts A and B are constructed in a significantly similar manner. Both texts consistently leave *something* out; neither text explicitly states whose interests are being protected. My reaction to the professor's comments indicates that I was not aware that my critique of the news story was written both to subsume the reporter's version of the *actual event* and to support the ideological practices of the shelter movement. Instead, I wrote as though I somehow knew the *truth* of the situation. My goal became conversion, not just rebuttal, of the reporter's version, a version which I neglected to locate in the specific realm of newspaper organization.

Neglecting to locate either text in a specific local history, I also neglected to explicate the organizational, ideological practices within which the news story was written (trick no. 1). I wrote, as the reporter also writes, to detach and separate ideas and to arrange them in an order which mystifies why either of us would be interested in a refuge shortage (trick no. 2). The difference between our positions is that the reporter writes in keeping with the mandates of the institution in which he works (ideological practices), whereas I, perhaps less consciously, wrote within the mandates of an ideology which remained unacknowledged.

Thus, using the tricks of mystification described above, I wrote in a way which individualizes my concern with a shelter shortage. In effect, I changed ideas into a person (trick no. 3). I wrote as if the individual reporter was responsible for obfuscating the refuge shortage problem. Similarly, the reporter wrote to individualize the problem, closing his article with the story of a lone battered woman who makes it on her own. Through these three tricks and the omission of certain *particulars* which make up the respective interpretive schemas, I was able to create, in keeping with the tenets of the documentary method of interpretation, a text in which "everything need not be said" (1982:30). The method I used to approach texts A and B is one which "consists of treating an actual appearance as 'the document of,' as 'pointing to,' as 'standing on behalf of' a presupposed underlying pattern . . ." (1982:24). As Smith's work so clearly demonstrates, this method of writing and researching produces a certain effect:

> The effect is peculiarly circular, for although questions of truth and falsity, accuracy and inaccuracy about the particulars may certainly be raised, the schema in itself is not called into question as a method of providing for the coherence of the collection of particulars as a whole (1982:25).

Conclusion
I have in this paper attempted to describe how I came to learn about the social organization of ideological practices through a botanizing exercise. The intent of my essay is to show how this exercise enabled me to examine the difference between (unconsciously) reproducing ideology and doing critical sociology. Specifically, I set out to examine the tension between texts B and C as a way of understanding the documentary character of text A. Using the professor's questions and comments as a point of departure, I began to see how I was able to work within *ideological boundaries* without a conscious realization of what I was doing. As a result of my work to complete the botanizing exercise, I began the long process of unbinding myself from the unconscious production of ideological practices. In so doing, I think I am better able to comprehend the *actual reality* (my boundedness to ideological practices) which I sought to understand but could not easily articulate without a dialogue between the texts in question and Smith's larger body of work.

My aim in reconstructing this series of effects is twofold: 1) I have sought to explain how Smith's scientific approach has altered my way of thinking and doing research, and 2) I would like to register what I consider the prime importance of the botanizing exercises. Like the work of other major thinkers, Smith's *ways* of working are not easily grasped. This is so, I think, because *she* developed these *ways*, in part as aspects of her own lived experiences, which differ from the experiences of other researchers. What Smith has produced, however, is a technique — the botanizing exercise — which I used to approach critically the ideological practices which make up a textual account. In my use of this technique, I as a researcher with my own question (what is missing?), entered into dialogue with Smith's way of thinking and doing research. From this *way* of doing research I learned how it is possible for researchers to move away from the bonds of ideological practices, and in so doing practice a more critical way of doing sociology.

C: (Some) Re-considerations

That was the way it was supposed to go, that was the way it had always gone before, but somehow it no longer felt right. I'd taken a wrong turn somewhere; there was something, some fact or clue, that I'd overlooked (Atwood, 1985).

I am trying to say that language embodies power never more strongly/magically than where it renders bodies powerless (Corrigan, 1987:7).

Anne Louise, do you think the gatekeepers of the academy are ready for me/you/us all (Becki Ross in Brookes, 1986:20)?

Dear Lily, Andrew and Virginia:

Orderly and tidy, this essay is testimony to my need to be *normal*: a (highly motivated) desire to write objectively in a manner which will please and convince others, a desire to do it right; and yet, a desire to cover the cracks and gaps when I am unable to do it right.

I completed essay two prior to writing about the abuses described and analyzed in Chapters 1 and 2. In part, I wrote the above essay because I was unable, initially, to produce an acceptable botanizing exercise. In the professor's words, there was *something missing* in my response. It was this missing something which seemed to prevent me from doing a *proper* reading.

Frustrated, I wrote the above essay to see if I might discover the missing something in my botanizing exercise. I wanted to do a proper reading. What I did not know when I began this exercise, however, is what a proper reading would entail. It would involve learning to write from my own perspective and authority towards making clear the social relations which organize the ideologies (mine included) in my reading of a selected newspaper article. The writing of essay two, therefore, enabled me to understand the assumption that ideology is a social construct. How?

As a result of writing the essay, re-working the first botanizing exercise, and re-reading the professor's comments, I began to understand her use of the term *proper*. I realized that her intent was to teach me to differently read the news accounts. In other words, her aim was for me to understand that our perspectives, mine and the reporter's, were nothing more than that: ideological perspectives. In working back through the problem presented to me by the professor, that something was missing in my reading — I understood, at one level, the intent of the botanizing exercise. In my opinion, her aim was to teach me to read in a way that would make clear how knowledges and ideologies are organized to represent vested interests rather than "truths".

While her perspective is now more obvious to me, this was not the case in my early attempts to understand the botanizing exercise. At the time, her assumption that ideology is a social construct was for me merely an abstraction. While writing essay two enabled me to move beyond this abstraction, it was not until I experienced the *deflation* of (male) authority within the context of another class that I began to see the professor's intent. I will discuss this other class following a brief discussion of 'the method'.

Key to the organization of essay two is my discovery of a new truth. I now know *the method* which taught me to understand ideology as a concept. In other words, in my attempt to demonstrate how I came to understand ideology, I, somewhat unconsciously, produce another truth claim: I have discovered *the method* for teaching others about ideology. Further, I claim that ideology is a perspective. Writing as if I have discovered the true method, I in fact obscure my ideological claim, that this is mine, and not necessarily the claim of Smith, whose method I purport to have discovered.

Leaving aside for a moment the question of whether an understanding of Smith's method is or is not a useful means for helping students understand ideology as a concept (which I think it is), I want to suggest that an application of Smith's method enabled me to examine differently one of the stories introduced in Chapter 4. This story revolves around the way in which my MA thesis advisor and I hung on to our differing notions of truth, neither of us able to view these notions as ideological perspectives. In retrospect, I think the botanizing exercise enabled me to see how and why we were each bound in our own ways by ideology. In knowing how ideology works, I came to understand the limitations of each of our perspectives and how I might move beyond them.

Thus, when speaking about the tendency to produce yet another truth perspective in essay two, I am not arguing with Smith's method, which I purport to understand. More mystically, I perhaps use essay two to convince an unnamed and unidentified audience of the truth of the method I have discovered. I, not Smith, was looking for a truth. That I do this within an academic context is not surprising. I had been taught well to believe that I must write to convince. As a student, I had been encouraged to test hypotheses. I had not been encouraged to highlight the limits I feel when I write. I had not been encouraged to write from my own authority. I had not been taught to write in a questioning manner. I wrote essay two to convince readers of the truth of the method which helped me to understand ideology as a concept.

Truth seeking is, of course, antithetical to Smith's aim to understand the social organization of individual perspectives. More importantly, key to Smith's method is an author's awareness of how she or he is an active participant in the reading and research process. In other words, Smith's is more than a critical method enabling readers to see how knowledge is organized. It is a method which implicitly demands authorial responsibility, accountability, and authority. In this way, authors must demonstrate how they, in relation to others, are producing and reproducing ideology: how, for whom, and why. I knew this at only one level when I wrote essay two. Also, I was not aware of the other factors enabling me to understand ideology as a social construct when I produced this paper. What are these other factors?

Rather than focus on the why or how of this question I will attempt to recall and reconstruct an event I now believe was key to the learning I describe in essay two. Specifically, I will discuss the graduate course I mentioned earlier and how I currently understand the importance of this course to the changes I describe in essay two.

The other course, like the one in which I learned to botanize, was for me a life-altering experience. My memory of writing an essay for this course is vivid; I produced it just prior to writing essay two. Vivid, too, are my memories of the teaching practices I observed and experienced in this course. Most vivid, however, is my memory of reclaiming and knowing my own authority as a writer through the joyous process of co-authoring an autobiographical paper with another student.

> Writing stories is fun. More than this, it expands our knowledge enormously, sharpens our social perception, improves our use of language, changes our attitude to others and to ourselves. It is a politically necessary form of cultural labour. It makes us live our lives more consciously (Haug et al., 1987:71).

For the duration of the other course I, with another student, first recognized as a problem, and then struggled with, our desire to produce a meaningful essay. More importantly, perhaps, we wanted to make the process meaningful. Over numerous coffees and breakfasts we tried to imagine how we might produce a paper which would better reflect our own interests (rather than the professor's) and our desire to write in an innovative way.

We decided to produce a collective essay in which we would "trace and articulate the multi-levelled implications" (Brookes and Ross, 1986:15) of our differing sexual identities as we were coming to know them. Excited by a method of presentation used in Hanscombe's (1982) novel *Between Friends* we decided to produce our essay in the form of a series of letters in which we would discuss our sexualities in relation to each other and to a variety of texts we were reading. Our intent was to write the collective essay in a two-week period.

The writing routine which we established for ourselves was radically different from that with which I had produced essay two. By contrast, we were invigorated and stimulated by the collective process. To begin, Becki wrote the first eight-page letter to me, after which we met and, over breakfast, discussed its contents. She then rested for twenty-four hours while I responded to her text in a second letter. Again, we met for breakfast and discussed our works. I rested and she wrote. We continued this process until satisfied that we had sufficiently addressed the theoretical issues as we had set out to do. Satisfied, we put our respective letters into one rather large document and off we went to deliver it to the course instructor. We were profoundly elated by the experience of producing a collective paper in this manner. In our opinion, it defied the lonliness of a *singly*-produced essay. In fact, because the process was so meaningful, its ending brought disappointment. To counteract our disappointment, we decided to form a larger collective writing group. During the next two years we met as a support group.

It is noteworthy that Becki and I did not request permission from the professor to write in a collective manner. Moreover, prior to delivering the essay we decided that because the production process was so meaningful to us, there was little the instructor, as a figure of authority, could say or do to make it any less meaningful, including giving us a poor grade for our work. We decided that a failing grade would simply reflect his perspective, not ours. In other words, his potential approval or disapproval was absolutely secondary to our experience. Our letters to one another had so significantly shifted our assumptions about writing forms and writing audiences that we could not imagine again producing a traditional essay.

I recount this story because it is significant when viewed in relationship to essay two, in which I describe my experience of learning to botanize. In fact, the collective method of producing an essay caused a conceptual shift which enabled me to know at a deep level the theory I had tried to understand in essay two. In other words, while I was learning to theorize (intellectually) ideology as a social construct, I was also experiencing this theory at another level because of the work —learning how to defy figures of authority and to create from my own perspective — which I was doing in the other class. I think the collective method of producing an essay enabled me to view myself in relationship to Becki as *real* authorities and producers of texts. In this way I began to reclaim an authority lost through abuse. Importantly, this re-learning of my own authority enabled me to internalize Smith's method: I was less controlled by the authority of others.

As a result of this experience, I attempt in my teaching practices to devise course requirements which enable students to work in less traditional, non-rote and more self-authoritative ways. These ways are key for learners whose relationships to authority have been disturbed.

The professor who received our collective essay also enhanced my sense of authority as a writer. In response to our letter-essay, he wrote thirty pages of comments indicating a respect for the work we had done. As a survivor of abuse who had learned to cope with a damaged relationship to authority, the experience of writing collectively, from my own perspective, changed how I relate to authority figures. This enabled me to learn anew.

I wrote essay two in the weekend following the completion of the collective project. Retrospectively, I find it interesting that I do not mention in that essay the other factors which contributed to my learning about ideology and knowledge as socially organized. In fact, I am not certain that I was aware of a connection between the work of these two courses. I will discuss this following a brief discussion of the professor's teaching practices in the other course.

This professor systematically engaged in a practice which I had not before experienced in a class taught by a male. Despite his reliance on the lecture mode, he nonetheless altered content presentation such that it dramatically shifted my usual response. Woven through his prepared lectures about theories of masculinity was his autobiographical reconstruction and recounting of his experience as a male. As a student attempting to understand ideology and knowledge as organized, I was helped by his conscious analysis of his struggle with the social construction of his own masculinity. I think, in fact, that his method of teaching through example showed me how to weave together theory and practice. Because of the intensity and emotion with which the material was shared and taught, I learned deeply about content and about how knowledge is produced and reproduced. This awareness, I think, enabled me to understand in greater depth the aims of the botanizing exercise.

The professors in the two courses were consistent in their respect for students' work. In their differing ways, each enabled me to begin a shift which eventually resulted in writing about my abuse. They taught me the validity of respectful teacher response, and to view teachers as resources and facilitators rather than as women and men able to wield considerable authority as teachers. As a survivor of abuse and a woman struggling in a male-organized world, this learning prepared me to begin writing from my own perspective.

Love and Solidarity.

In my opinion, letter-writing is a useful way of organizing academic work. Similarly, I argue the importance of writing from an autobiographical perspective. These forms are important because they enable writers to regard and address readers from the perspective of responsibility and care rather than the detachment most commonly encouraged in academe. Importantly, too, these methods may be used to teach students to become authorities of their own perspectives. This learning is key to understanding ideology as a social construct. For abuse survivors these methods are important because they teach students to consciously reclaim lost authority. In Chapter 7, I will discuss how a third essay similarly affected my learning.

chapter seven

A: Reading From the Margins

The principle task of feminist criticism, in providing a necessary re-vision of the politics of "truth", is to make its own ideology explicit. If we seek to transform the structures of authority, we must first name them, and in doing so, unmask and expose them for all to see (Meese, 1986:16).

Writing is a transgression of boundaries, an exploration of new territory. It involves making public the events of our lives, wriggling free of the constraints of purely private and individual experiences. From a state of modest insignificance we enter a space in which we can take our-selves seriously (Haug et al., 1987:36).

Essay two, which I introduced in Chapter 6, marks a major shift in my learning. I think it signals my coming to terms with ideologies as concepts which constitute bodies of knowledge. To know ideologies as concepts is to know, therefore, that concepts are developed by real people. This is to know, then, that concepts are changeable. To know that concepts and ideas are changeable is to know that knowledge is socially constructed. To know this is to be able to critique the fact that knowledge is organized to benefit different people in different ways. At the level of theory, this is a straightforward idea. At the level of practice, it is not so straightforward. For example, I had learned to regard ideologies and knowledges as abstractions rather than practices due to my experiences of abuse. This way of learning is reinforced by main-stream schooling practices, and because of it, I learned to silence the experiences which shape and inform me still.

Why should it make a difference to know how knowledge is socially constructed and organized? At one level, it is difficult to explain how I learned to believe that the abuse done to me was not important and did not affect me. Similarly, it is difficult to explain how I assumed the abuse to be my fault or how I learned that I was not safe to speak about the causes of my fears. At another level, it is easy to explain my silence. Throughout my many years of schooling, apart from the work I did in a feminist-oriented context, I encountered not one teacher who taught me to critique the relations of power which enable men to violate women. Not one teacher was willing to critique harassment, rape or sexual abuse from a woman's perspective. Never, in a schooling context, was I exposed to a text in a manner which would enable me to critique the abuses done to me, nor was I taught to know the constructedness of such concepts as femininity and masculinity. Not one adult taught me that women are not necessarily safe in their own homes. Instead, I was taught the illusion that I would be cared for, and protected, by men.

In other words, I was taught an ideology of social relations which prevented me from examining and knowing the oppression and powerlessness of women. This same ideology, of course, also prevents men from knowing how they are taught to oppress and misuse power. Because women and men are taught to uncritically live the ideology of social inequality, albeit in differing ways, it is therefore very difficult for women and men to learn to critique illusions — which work like truths when one is not taught to critique them — for the purpose of imagining better ways of relating to each other. Traditions are reproduced in this same manner, I suggest.

I did not know about ideology as a concept, thus I did not (really) know my brother's abuse as abuse; instead I felt only the effects because a) I had not been taught to think critically; b) I did not know to critique the abuses done to me because I was bound both ideologically and by a learned body fear to the trauma of abuse; c) being bound by trauma further prevented my ability to think critically, because I could not learn or know from my own authority or perspective. Imprisoned by the authority of my brother and a male-organized society, I found it difficult to critique my abuse from other than his perspective, constructed in silence, power, and privilege; and d) unable to critique my silence, and his power and privilege to name the abuse (my fault, my problem, not important), I learned to exist, to survive, rather than to create, produce and critique. Within the framework of my brother, and that of a male-organized society, it was under-

standably difficult for me to know myself as a producer of knowledge. Thus, because I learned as a woman the difficulties in altering both my private and public circumstances, I also learned to think of ideology as an abstraction. To know otherwise is a freeing, albeit dangerous, experience.

*In Chapter 7, my aim is to introduce a third, autobiographical, essay which marks my attempts to put into practice the theories described in Chapter 6. While at one level Chapter 6 represents my attempts to unbind myself theoretically from the limitations of uncritiqued ideologies, at another level it represents a practical attempt to unbind myself from the effects of an abuse I had not yet **recognized** or spoken about publicly when I produced essay three. Theoretical and practical binds are, of course, interrelated. I think, however, that I found it difficult to recognize or speak about this abuse because I was unable to simultaneously critique and emotionally re-experience the abuse. I will return to this discussion in my next letter.*

Essay three was written several months prior to my decision to alter my thesis and to write about abuse. In my opinion, this essay, constructed as part of the requirement for a graduate course, represents a significant shift in my learning. Through identification with the narrator in Gilman's text, I began to see better how relations of power differently organize women and men. I began to imagine how I might remove myself from the bonds of a male-organize society through critique, writing and speech.

Introduced in this course to reader-response theory, I discovered the intricate connections of reader-responses to the production of knowledge. Having just begun to know myself (really) as a producer of knowledge and because of my long-standing love of reading, I was elated to be taking this course. Importantly, my reading of Gilman's The Yellow Wallpaper *(1973, originally published in 1892), a text which I read in the context of the course, had a profound effect upon me. In Chapter 8, I will discuss how Gilman's text prepared me to write about my experiences of abuse.*

Dear Lily, Andrew and Virginia:

While much of the classroom experience in which essay three was constructed was positive and exciting for me, much was also painful and disturbing. Positively, I was so excited by the reading material for this course that I read far beyond the requirements, immersing myself in a subject area quite unusual to sociology. This experience was shared by a number of other women in the class with whom I met and discussed the material, often apart from the classroom. Much of what I learned from this class is now an important part of my teaching practice. In view of the fact that I attempted to write and think in a more open-ended way, to move away from claiming truths and definite answers, and creating closures, I was at times frustrated by what I perceived to be the professor's canon-oriented, non-sociological approach to texts. Given my background in sociology and education, I did not read to talk about characters, per se. Rather, I read to discover how characters affect me and others: I read to know better the everyday practices of ordinary people, such as Charlotte Perkins Gilman who lived and wrote over one hundred years ago.

Gilman wrote *The Yellow Wallpaper* (1973), a fictionalized autobiographical account, in part to free herself from years of suffering from "a severe and continuous nervous breakdown tending to melancholia—and beyond" (Lane, 1980:19). She also wrote to free herself from the madness of marriage, and from the medical authorities who maintained that her well-being depended upon her willingness to live a quiet, domestic life, and most of all to not write, the assumption being that writing made her ill. Contrary to all authority other than her own she nonetheless chose to write. Indeed, she wrote herself well.

As a survivor of abuse, I identified strongly with the narrator in *The Yellow Wallpaper*, an imprisoned woman artist silenced by marriage and medicine, and reduced to the status of a little girl without a name. The narrator had to (metaphorically) remove the yellow wallpaper from her bedroom walls to secure freedom. Freedom meant finally identifying the ideological frameworks and institutions which imprisoned her. It meant knowing her feelings of madness to be the 'actual' madness of the male-organized culture in which she lived.

Like Gilman, I sensed that I had to write to name the structures of authority which imprisoned me. And like Haug et al., I would indeed learn that "Writing is a transgression of boundaries" (1987:36) which, once transgressed, would empower me to begin taking myself seriously (3). Reading Gilman, I began to imagine, to see, to feel, that many of my private and individual fears were perhaps not private and individual but in fact, social. With this in mind, I invite you to read beyond the work of essay three to an analysis of how *The Yellow Wallpaper* (1973) prepared me further to write about my experiences of abuse.

Love and Solidarity.

B: Writing from the Margins

Beginnings and Endings:
One Reader Reading The Yellow Wallpaper

<Essay Three>

Literature is no one's private ground; literature is common ground. Let us trespass freely fearlessly and find our way for ourselves (Woolf, 1938).

One of the most blatant contradictions in discourses surrounding the more emancipatory and contemporary literary criticism, i.e. reader-response criticism, feminist literary criticism, is that the recognition of *reader power* (Belsey, 1980) has in some ways resulted in an initial paralysis of the reader manifested in the *where does one begin?* syndrome. The internal struggles I, as this reader about to embark upon this reading of *The Yellow Wallpaper*, must confront are compounded by my previous readings, for example that which I presented recently in a graduate seminar course; and by my reading/hearing of present others' readings as well as my reading of non-present others whose *scholarly* readings will be used, unfortunately but necessarily, to add legitimacy to my own work.

Having focused for some time on this struggle over beginnings, I have decided to start with the same struggle, that is to construct a reading of *The Yellow Wallpaper* which takes seriously what may be one of Gilman's most powerful and over-riding messages: that meaning, sense, knowledge, and in this case, madness, are socially organized practices. I hope to at least partially accomplish this by showing the ways in which the female narrator of the story sees her own constructed and (mis)read insanity/madness and how this *seeing* may be analogous to the experience of those forced to read in tightly constrained, highly elitist and extremely sexist ways which resist the notion of reader as meaning-maker, producer of text, constructor of personal, yet socially representative, knowledge.

Other readers have alluded to some of the ways in which Gilman's *The Yellow Wallpaper* poses this, now very timely but still very radical, argument. Rachel Blau Duplessis, referring to the way Gilman constructs the ending of the story to the ending's open-end/edness, makes the following claim:

> At the ending, depending on one's interpretive paradigm, two contradictory opinions about the main character can be held. The conflicting judgments are simultaneously present, as the narrator, tearing the wallpaper, tries to release her double, the muted subtext with its unsaid meanings. "Much madness is divinest sense" here. But from the standpoint of "Much Sense — the starkest Madness" — that is, from the perspective of *normality* (italics mine), her statement demanding freedom for the muted meanings looks like irrationality and delusion. By an ending that calls attention to interpretive paradigms and powers, Gilman highlights the politics of narrative (1985:92-93).

As Duplessis has succeeded in pointing out, Gilman's ending forcefully throws into question any notions of normal stability, madness and, yes, meaning. And it is not only the sexual politics of interpretation addressed through such an ending. Where oftentimes the struggle over the word becomes a struggle for a *truth*, textual politics generally get played out on the terrain of fiction of which interpretation, without a call to *truth* or determinate meaning, is a part. The protagonist/narrator's struggle at the end of The Yellow Wallpaper is a strong analogy to readers for whom meanings are muted by *interpretive paradigms* which lay exclusive claim to stable texts and absolute meaning. How Gilman shows the insanity of this stance is terrifying.

Kolodny focuses her discussion of The Yellow Wallpaper in a manner similar to how I have chosen in this essay to respond to Gilman. Kolodny, in A Map of Rereading, first establishes the basis of her argument around "the fact that whether we speak of poets and critics *reading* texts or writers *reading*, and thereby recording for us, the world, we are calling attention to interpretive strategies that are learned, historically determined, and thereby necessarily gender-inflected" (1985:47). Employing Bloom's notion of *misprision* or misreading, she goes on to say, again in particular relation to the ending of The Yellow Wallpaper, that

> Gilman's story represents not so much an object for the recurrent misreadings, or misprisions, of readers and critics (though this, of course, continues to occur) as an exploration, within itself, of the gender-inflected interpretive strategies responsible for our mutual misreadings, and even horrific misprisions, across sex lines (Kolodny, 1985:54).

It also seems clear to me as a reader that Gilman's narrator is a character whose *raison d'etre* is to divulge the madness of the patriarchal institutions of marriage and medicine, of how these institutions are constructed to oppress, and of how socially organized yet deeply mystified and naturalized *knowledge* is powerfully implicated in this oppression. That the narrator from the very beginning discloses that "one expects that" her husband, John, a doctor, will laugh at her ideas and that his being a physician is "perhaps one reason I do not get well faster" (Gilman, 1973:3) speaks clearly to the gender-based, inferior positioning of her thoughts and to her awareness of how dominant male thought defines her *in sanity*, insane.

Gilman's ever-partial statement of intent concerning *The Yellow Wallpaper* seems to contribute to this assumption. Written after suffering a (so-called) nervous breakdown for which her male physician prescribed that she "live as domestic a life as possible" read, "fulfil your male-defined proper role of good wife and mother"; "have but two hours' intellectual life a day" read, "do not think; especially do not challenge male ideas"; and "never to touch pen, brush or pencil again" read, "be silent, women's stories do not count", Gilman's story is devastatingly mocking. In all my readings of *The Yellow Wallpaper*, one impression has remained: I am struck from the beginning by the madness/anger of a sane narrator pitted against a passively oppressive and harmful, perhaps insane, male-defined and dominated world.

I do not include Gilman's statement of intent here to limit interpretation but rather to indicate part of the textuality out of which my reading came. I am especially sensitive to this aspect of Gilman's text given recent personal experiences with the male medical profession, in which my womanly body/mind was terrorized by gender-biased prognoses and diagnoses. That, too, is part of the text of my response to the story and I mention it as but one tiny episode which suggests that the yellow wallpaper *madness* which gripped Gilman and her narrator is not so very different from the madness I encounter in my daily life as a feminist, and as a woman living in a world organized largely by men.

There is, of course, much within the *actual text* with which a reader can play in what Barthes (1979) refers to as the playful production of meaning, the pleasure of the text. As a reader, and a feminist reader at that, I cannot ideologically separate this subject position. In fact, I like to think that my feminist perspective provides me with a a fuller subject position from which to approach *The Yellow Wallpaper*. It is worth noting that, since being published in 1892 and billed in subsequent reprintings as "a horror story," this text did not receive a feminist (re) reading until 1973 (Lane, 1980:xvii). As Russ points out, such false categorizing is, at its worst, the deliberate re-naming of phenomena so as to change their significance (1983:49). Calling *The Yellow Wallpaper* a horror story may well capture a sense of how feminists would receive it today; however, at the turn of the century such categorization most certainly prevented it from being read by those who would have benefited, in anger and revolt, from it most. In this sense, I claim my own reading of this *horror story* as, indeed, enabled by the social and historical movement which is feminism, still struggling for a literary history, a literary voice, at present.

That is not to suggest or imply, however, that feminist readings of *The Yellow Wallpaper* are unanimous. Even those with similar ideological interests or interests couched under the same non-homogeneous umbrella term read differently. Class, race, and age are only a few of the factors contributing to this diversity, factors which Joanna Russ calls "the historical facts of what it is to be female or black or working class or what-have-you" (1983:120). To acknowledge one such different reading of Gilman's story in comparison to my own, both of which could claim to be feminist readings, I shall address the conclusion by Delany that *The Yellow Wallpaper* is "a story of defeat" (1983:165).

To begin, I am not convinced that referring to it as a story of defeat is really different, on a certain level, from calling it a horror story. Immediately, it is necessary to question the assumptions these readers are making about horror and defeat. For me, horror is the pervasive horror of a male-organized society, not the horror of insanity. Defeat is too petrifying for me to accept as an adequate description of the overall tone of the story. From where I, as a reader, am located, *The Yellow Wallpaper* is not a story of defeat, but rather one of victory and emancipation. This claim is obviously not unconnected to my earlier reading of the narrator, whom I am convinced is aware, from the beginning, of the patriarchal forces paralysing her. To refer to this story as a defeatist account of a woman's descent into madness seems to miss the point and actually succumbs to the very construction of insanity which *The Yellow Wallpaper* presents problematically. What Gilman and her narrator are saying to me is that this particular liberation is achieved, not at the cost of or through the madness of the narrator, but at the cost of re-defining the whole notion of madness itself.

I find it helpful here to address the stance taken by Kolodny that in *The Yellow Wallpaper*, "liberation here is liberation only into madness" (1985:54), by which Kolodny refers to the madness of the text/diary that is the story. This madness is the encasement of her liberation of her *other*, set free by the removal of the wallpaper, into the printed word. While I can see Kolodny's point, I disagree with it, for it suggests an elitist and intimidating view of language and texts; that is, they constitute a powerful mystification out of which meaning can never be fully derived: thus the madness, the wallpaper which can never be completely removed. While this is almost certainly the case, or at least the case of the theory of texts and response which I advocate here, Kolodny's madness can only be madness if full, determinate, stable meaning is a goal of interpretation. If it isn't, there is no madness, only play.

Unless readers, like Kolodny, accept the integrity of other readers' interpretations, and with that their sometime ability to read in a liberatory way, for the narrator, then the construction of meaning remains fixated within dominant paradigms, not unlike the normality which threatens to suffocate the narrator of *The Yellow Wallpaper*. Somewhat arrogantly, I would like to assert that my present reading of Gilman's story is liberatory in the sense that it recognizes the constraints within which the narrator lives and suffers but does not judge her for how she, as an individual, acts out both her accommodations of male organizations and her resistance, not separate from her so-called madness in/sanity, to those same constraints. It is this same accommodation and resistance which goes on not only in the ways women live their lives within a male-organized society but also in the ways in which readers read.

This idea of accommodation and resistance is one of the most significant and provocative conclusions Radway (1984) reaches in her study of women reading mass-produced romance novels. Even in the seemingly overwhelming acceptance and reproduction of patriarchy implicit in the romance, this accommodation is not necessarily completely carried over into the reading of a romance which, as a social practice in women's lives, is a point of resistance in itself. Duplessis alludes to this unusual, in 1892, representation of resistance by female characters in fiction when she notes the transitional nature of Gilman's texts: "Instead of submitting to . . . complicity or battered resignation . . Gilman's hero performs the act signalling a shift in female narrative politics" (1985:91). This is exciting when seen in the act of reading; but, as Duplessis notes, seen in the image of a character such as the narrator of *The Yellow Wallpaper*, it is especially significant and equally exciting.

To speak about a character as I have just spoken of the narrator of the story is not really to talk about the character, per se, but rather about the way my particular reading of this character affected me, moved me, and in some way acted as an agent in my articulation of specific feelings around marriage, medicine and madness in particular, and male-organized society in general. In other words, I am not so much speaking about the text of *The Yellow Wallpaper* as I am about the effect this text, the character of the narrator in particular, has had on my life as a feminist woman reader. This is a deliberate act on my part, which I can explain in two ways, each related to how I have chosen to respond to Gilman's story.

First of all, it is always more important for me to think about and feel the effects of reading a specific text than it is to discuss how the text might or might not succeed as a *work of art*. While such responses may be important to critics with vested capitalistic and ideological interests in promoting such discriminatory reading, these practices seem far removed from the lives of individuals reading in differently interested ways. As Belsey suggests, such practice promotes an outrageously oppressive sensibility in a select group of readers, who use it as "the source of its right to control and administer experience" (1982:129). My concern here is to convey my experience and reading of *The Yellow Wallpaper* as not separate from the contamination of various ideological influences, but in acknowledgement of the not-so-innocent nature of reading.

Closely related to my argument about the effects of a text in my life and with a reader's response to a text in her or his life, is a refusal to inadvertently give legitimacy to textual analysis which claims a distanced, critical reading of a text. Such readings are reminiscent of a form of dissection in which the reader is a scientist with varying degrees of (in)ability. Those readings reflect little of what *The Yellow Wallpaper* could mean in a specific person's life. In the name of literariness, however, such readings can and do result in a censoring of important texts, many of them written by women. Where such texts manage to prevail in patriarchy, marginal (feminist) readings are often silenced, allowing for such (mis)readings as those which kept *The Yellow Wallpaper* categorized as a horror story. It is thus my own *moment of resistance* to avoid such close textual analysis and to persist instead in addressing the construction of meaning and response as I see it played out in Gilman's story.

There are, however, very powerful images constructed in Gilman's story with which I interact in intense and significant ways. That is, certain images inform the reading I am now engaged in more than in others. Earlier readings, for example my seminar reading, were sometimes informed by different images, or images read in a different way, or images positioned differently in terms of their significance in my construction of a specific reading response. By acknowledging this partiality of the text, I also acknowledge the partial nature of all of my readings and any reading, for that matter, of *The Yellow Wallpaper* or any text. This also puts aside the notion of a complete, coherent text, or reading, and rejects the usual goal of criticism, that of "closing the text" (Belsey, 1980:109), instead leaving texts and readings always open.

Thus, in this reading, I work with particular *images*, some already obvious in my discussion so far, such as the ending and the character of the narrator. Neither of these can be really separated from the way I read the grand patriarch of husband/doctor John, who works to enclose the narrator in marriage and madness. Focusing on his voice throughout the story has a profoundly comic effect as his incipient *madness* is revealed in my feminist reading. Indeed, reading his patriarchal madness is one means by which I perceive the sanity of the narrator and the ingenuity of the ending of *The Yellow Wallpaper*. It is a classic case of marital oppression, reflected in a number of actual reversals: the bedroom, a site of trust and exchange becomes a prison cell; the husband/partner becomes the patriarch/oppressor; medicine becomes poison; *sisterhood* becomes complicity with patriarchy; and, of course, madness becomes sanity. This last reversal, in which I am able to view the madness of the seemingly sane, is made possible through the challenges to normality in the first four reversals.

How these particular, in a sense dominant, images work in the construction of this response is most obvious when I think about and respond to the over-riding image which is the text itself, the diary which the narrator writes along with the reader. The "heavy opposition" (4) which the narrator knows her secretive writing will meet, a point constantly repeated in the diary, has the effect of creating a patriarchal shadow which hovers over the text and permeates my interaction with *The Yellow Wallpaper*. The imprisoned woman artist, silenced by marriage and medicine, reduced to a little girl without a name, effaced by the yellow wallpaper madness of patriarchy, does manage to free herself and regain her voice. This is epitomized not only by the ending of the story but in the concrete existence of the diary/text. It is in a similar sense that I struggle under the shadow of male-organized literary theory to have my own different reading(s) of *The Yellow Wallpaper* heard in this essay.

The preceding point is where this essay began. Long before I had ever read *The Yellow Wallpaper*, I was convinced by reading other texts that what we call novels or fictions can be highly theoretical reading. I am also convinced that *theory* can be highly fictional. Whether or not such categorizations can ever again be defended in light of deconstructionist theories is uncertain. Nevertheless, I read *The Yellow Wallpaper* as a story which in its very telling is a theoretical argument about the social organization of reality, about the determinants of that construction, how it is to live on the margins of a reality organized to negate your interests, and how it is possible to resist, on some level, the practices of that oppression. Charlotte Perkins Gilman once remarked that "it is no easy matter to deny or reverse a universal assumption" (Lane, 1980:21). Questioning such *universal* assumptions as are present in male-organized society is not very different than questioning and challenging assumptions about universal truths, absolute meaning, literary canons. It is this *theoretical* statement I see being powerfully made in Gilman's *The Yellow Wallpaper*.

There is a sense in which my reading of *The Yellow Wallpaper* is more about my struggle to construct and communicate a reading. I began this essay by addressing the struggle around beginnings; the struggle around endings is no less crucial for me as a reader, as shadows and fears of closure raise their ugly heads. *The Yellow Wallpaper* has a provocative and open ending, and to close an essay on it with a less than open ending would be contradictory to the text and to my reading of it (which is already different, even as I write these last words). It is because of this desire for *open-endedness* that I stop writing this so-called ending: I invite readers to share with me your readings of *The Yellow Wallpaper*.

C: An(other) Feminist Analysis of the Fallout

Opening spaces where we, readers marginalized by gender, sexuality, class, race, age and region, can reclaim our voices has always been one of the primary concerns of a critical pedagogy (Kelly, 1986:5).

Dear Lily, Andrew and Virginia:

While a course taught by a woman does not necessarily include as part of its agenda a feminist project of any kind, this one did. For this reason I, like other class participants, anticipated a *safe* setting, one in which the struggle to be heard would not be marked by relations of power as most "male-stream" (O'Brien, 1981) graduate courses. But, alas, the "patriarchal shadow" (Brookes, 1986) loomed large, dark and sometimes ominous, constantly reminding me to question my feelings of safety within the academic classroom.

It was thus that I struggled in this course. No shared concern, feminist or otherwise, was ever fully articulated, and as theoretical collision overrode coalescence, the class was factionalized to the extent that any feminist project was marginalized. Feminists were those of us who could not read 'literary' texts a certain (read correct) way, clearly demonstrated by the degree of resistance to alternative feminist readings. These readings, those in opposition argued, were blurred by ideology and politics, as if all other readings were somehow virginal and unmarred by those factors which shape our every social relation, reading included. This was difficult for me to comprehend in a course that at the same time introduced me to reader response criticism, which helped me value theoretically my own reader agency.

Highly enthused by this approach, and given my love of texts, I set out to read and critique *The Yellow Wallpaper* from a perspective which would make sense of how gender relations are socially organized. In this case, I wanted to examine Gilman's assumptions about socially constructed madness; my aim was to,

> construct a reading of *The Yellow Wallpaper* which takes seriously what may be considered one of Gilman's most powerful and over-riding messages — that meaning, sense, knowledge (in this case, madness) are socially constructed (Brookes, 1986:2).

My intent was to explicate the narrator's awareness of the constructedness of her situation, and to suggest how her experience of madness was somewhat analogous to my feelings of madness. When first reading Gilman's text, I was not ready to know or speak about the ways in which I was affected by my history of abuse. Nonetheless, I think I was being prepared in a variety of ways to confront this abuse.

Many factors prepared me for my confrontation with abuse. Key to this was my decision to work in a feminist-oriented environment where I was privileged to study with scholars working from feminist perspectives, perspectives I could use to critique the relations of power, social oppression and inequality organizing my everyday experiences. This critique, I think, is crucial to my ongoing recovery from abuse. It is a long and slow recovery. This should not be surprising, given the long-term effects of traumas in a society in which children and adults are not systematically taught to critique experience from the perspective of relations of power.

Abuse paralysed me. It made me afraid to critique. It taught me to fear making choices based on my own needs and desires because for many years I lived with the unconscious dread that I would be 'found out'. In this way I stayed in the grip of my brother's authority, with my unnamed fears, in the shadow of a society organized to unevenly empower women and men. In a very practical way my fears controlled me. They prevented me from thinking that I could do the work of teaching, despite the fact that I was preparing myself for this work. And, as a result of abuse and trauma, I learned to fear writing.

A constant in the work you are reading is my fear of writing. Earlier, I suggested that this is related to a fear of 'telling'. At another level, I think my fear of writing is directly related to not knowing my own authority, an authority stolen first through abuse and later through learning to write as a woman in a male-organized society, where I had, in Patsy's terms, to ghostwrite. As a ghostwriter I learned to distrust my own writing. I *felt* that what I wrote did not describe my reality or my expectations but rather the expectations of male experience. This feeling is, I suggest, a kind of *madness*. Not able to describe my reality, I learned, as do many women and men (in differing ways) to hide in my texts. I wrote as an alien. Concretely, I learned to *slip in* ideas important to me.

I was not aware that I had learned the practice of *slipping in* my perspectives until two teachers, both working from feminist perspectives, pointed this out to me. Prior to their critique of my writing practices, I was not consciously aware that I did not write from my own named perspectives; nor was I aware that I *slipped in* ideas. I did not understand what it meant to write from my own perspective. I did not understand what it might mean to exist in my own text except at the level of abstraction and theory.

In my reading of *The Yellow Wallpaper*, I responded emotionally to the narrator's desire to liberate herself through writing. I was fascinated by her idea of writing an autobiographical, fictionalized critique for the purpose of freeing herself from the madness of her circumstances. As a child I had learned, on one hand, that stories and books are indispensable to my emotional well-being: reading has enabled me to survive. Novels, in particular, help me to live and to imagine new possibilities. Reading stories enables me to enter other peoples' struggles, and to discover ways to reorganize my own experience. Until recently, however, I had read few novels which explained my experiences of abuse. On the other hand, I had read few theory texts which helped to explain my experience. And when I did read theories about abuse, I was unable to identify with the same emotion, enthusiasm and joy with which I read novels. In many respects I had learned to read theory as an abstraction rather than as of possible value to me.

I think I first became conscious of this difference while in the course in which I read with considerable emotion Gilman's *Yellow Wallpaper* (1973) in conjunction with less emotional readings of theoretical texts supporting the ideas described and critiqued by Gilman. It was this combined way of reading (similar ideas expressed in differing ways), an approach I commonly use to organize my classroom practices, which taught me how to experience a concept, idea or ideology in an emotional way. To do otherwise, as pointed out in conversation with Kathleen Rockhill, is to read theories and texts which in no way touch or affect us.

For survivors of abuse and, I would add, survivors of any kind of trauma (which includes most of us), I think it is imperative that we emotionally experience both the old ideologies and theories which bound us to the trauma and alternatives to the trauma. In other words, I think we need to re-experience trauma in a safe environment in order to move beyond it. For example, in my reading of Gilman I was able to identify emotionally with the narrator as well as with Gilman's 'novel' critique of a male-organized society. When these same ideas were reinforced in so-called theoretical accounts, I learned to critique the ideas in Gilman's work, because I was experiencing them at both the levels of abstraction and emotion. It was this way of critiquing which I later used to examine, feel and analyze my own history of abuse. I was aided by my simultaneous immersion in feminist-oriented theoretical perspectives. Thus, from a theoretical position based on emotional experience, I began to replace outmoded practices with new. I was not yet ready, however, to write and speak about my own abuse. Instead I wrote essays which suggested a state of readiness, on one hand, and a continuing state of retreat and resistance, on the other. It would take many months for me to name my own abuse. In fact, I did not choose to speak until two teachers publicly discussed their own experiences of abuse.

In my re-reading of the essays introduced in Chapters 5 through 7, I am mildly shocked by my feeling of disconnectedness from them. I find it difficult, for example, to identify with the way I wrote the essays. I feel as if I am the ghostwriter of my own stories. I wrote as an alien, both to myself and to the male-organizied society.

Despite the style used to organize these three essays, each was written with intense emotion. In all cases I identified, at one level, emotionally and theoretically with the accounts. At another level, I had not learned to reproduce theory-based emotion. In other words, I had learned well after years of study, and as a result of abuse, to deny emotion, to write without emotion, particularly in an academic context. One could not be emotional and objective. From this perspective it was difficult to write about ideas and practices which really matter to me. Thus I learned (again) to hide in my writing. I learned to borrow the ideas and words of others and to use them as a lens through which I glimpsed my own experiences and ideas. This need for a lens is why I begin each of my chapters with quotes.

To look through the eyes of another is not a problem if, in fact, we eventually learn how we are organized to see in particular ways. For example, my critique of essay one enabled me to recognize a key practice in my own social history — that of absenting myself, which I learned as a result of abuse — though at the time of writing essay one I was not prepared to make this connection and, instead, applied this concept to an analysis of battered women. Also, Woolf's theoretical analysis of male-organized practices touched deeply my desire to critique male-organized structures.

I wrote essay two because I passionately wanted to understand ideology as a concept. I sensed that this was important, as indeed it proved to be. Essay two is also important, in that during the time I was learning to theorize ideology, I was simultaneously exerting resistance to academic authority by writing my part of a collective paper. When reading *The Yellow Wallpaper* (1973) for essay three, I felt another kind of resistance: that I could and must escape the madness of my own social history.

I think the work of these three essays, written in a relatively safe environment and with the loving support of a dear friend, empowered me to begin a long process of self-discovery. I had been taught to hide from myself in a society organized to prevent me from seeing my own abuse. Like Gilman's narrator, I was learning that there was more behind the yellow wallpaper than I had been taught to see.

Following completion of my course work and the writing of essay three, several months passed before I began to confront, in writing, a social history organized by abuse and fear. The crisis which lead to this confrontation occurred in the context of two academics speaking publicly about their respective experiences of abuse. Hearing their words, hearing the emotion with which they spoke, and witnessing the embodiment of their pain was for me the pivotal moment. I decided then to begin my own process of confrontation.

In the weeks following this confrontation, I knew that I had to use my thesis to write about my abuse and I knew that I had to do it in a non-traditional way. I knew that I had to emotionally re-experience the abuse in order to re-interpret it. In this way I would change my learned understanding of my experience. Though terrified, the elation I felt as I began to write proved to be stronger than fear. Moved by desire and an intense pleasure I had never before felt in a writing context, I began my autobiographical thesis. I also began to teach for the first time. I was thrilled to discover my feeling of comfort in the classroom. I began to know a new sense of wellness. Like the narrator of *The Yellow Wallpaper* (1973) I had, at one level, escaped.

Love and Solidarity.

The teacher for whom essay three was produced had no way of knowing my social history. Unless she devised methods and practices to validate a way of studying English by bringing together theory and practice, she would never know, nor would I, how and why the work of this essay was important to me. While a participant in her class, I was unable to confront my experiences of abuse. Thus, much of that time I experi-

enced as fearful. She, of course, could not know what shaped my fear of writing, or my fear of authority figures, women included. As a survivor of abuse, it was, however, key to my learning that she attempted to familiarize herself with feminist perspectives on social inequality and relations of power; that she worked continuously to share her authority; and that she struggled with students to create a safe learning environment. Her failures, like mine, are the product of a society organized around methods of learning which can damage women and men in profound ways.

In this chapter I examined some of the ways I was prevented from knowing my own experience of abuse. My aim was to demonstrate the necessity of teaching students to critique the multitude of social factors organizing their social histories. I suggested further that students learn better to critique social practices when they are encouraged to approach theory in an emotional way. To do this does not demand, as assumed by Belenky et al. (1986), the creation of yet another model of education, particularly one for women only. Rather, based on my experiences in the classroom and as an autobiographical writer, I think we can effectively use our existing classrooms to alter the educational experience.

chapter eight

A: Some End(ings)

So much for endings. Beginnings are always more fun. True connoisseurs, however, are known to favour the stretch in between, since it's the hardest to do anything with. That's about all that can be said for plots, which anyway are just one thing after another, a what and a what and a what. Now try How and Why (Atwood, 1983:40).

Recovering the subject and the subject matter may sometimes be shocking and painful . . . . A disinterested and dispassionate discourse does not give life to its subject matter. On the contrary it seeks to deny the validity of the subject matter and to silence the subject (Paget,1987:22).

Chapter 7 is a discussion of my reactions and responses to Charlotte Perkins Gilman's book The Yellow Wallpaper (1973). In Chapter 8 my aim is to discuss briefly some of the ways I construct myself into the production of this text. I wrote as a means of understanding how my learning is shaped by experiences of abuse. My plan was to reconstruct and analyze a variety of stories and essays to better understand how I was affected by abuse; and how I was taught to reproduce abuse in a schooling context. My interest in this project stems from my desire to move beyond the effects of abuse, as well as to offer a partial critique of schooling practices from my understanding of feminist pedagogies.

I began this work struggling with a personal contradiction. Could I legitimately study the experiences of battered women without examining my own abuse? Following a series of crises, I chose to write an autobiographical thesis from which to examine my abuse. I made this choice because I sensed that I could not engage in active research with others until I had examined closely the traumas, assumptions and ideologies which shaped so many of my decisions and behaviours, including how I engage in research practices. I chose to write in an autobiographical mode because, while I intended to theorize my experience of abuse, I did not want to construct this theory in a non-feeling manner: I did not want to deny emotionally that which I was describing and analyzing. I also felt that an autobiographical approach would enable me to re-experience the trauma and ostensibly move me beyond its effects. Lastly, I chose to construct my text in the form of letters, in which I reconstructed and analyzed personal stories, events, and essays, for the purpose of developing a theoretical perspective with which to understand the effects of abuse.

Dear Lily, Andrew and Virginia:

What you have just read is one version of how I imagine I learn and develop and why I imagine it makes a difference to speak about my experiences of abuse. From selected stories, essays, events, practices, gaps and omissions, this is my first attempt to examine in an emotion-based, theoretical way a social history which I learned to forget and to *not know*. Writing autobiographically, my intent is to begin to *disentangle* myself from a social history which continues to inform and shape me.

Working from a perspective well articulated in Weedon's (1987) quote in the Preamble to this work, I aim to critique some of the ways in which abuse disturbed my self-identity as a producer of knowledge, making it difficult for me to comprehend the assumption that knowledge is socially constructed and organized.

Specifically, I examine how I learned, as an abuse survivor, to depend upon external authority rather than on the internal authority of my own needs and desires. Denied, through abuse, the authority of my own perspective, my intent was to analyze how I had learned to reproduce the illusions of a male-organized society. In a similar way I wrote to understand how I had accepted and reproduced schooling practices which legitimate linear and objective forms; and how I had learned to write in dispassionate and disinterested ways. This manner of writing further separated and divided me from myself, from others, and from knowledge of how these illusions produce and reproduce social divisions. Thus, I use this book to begin breaking free of the illusions which perpetuated in me a sense of oppression and learned helplessness.

In doing this, I attempt to disrupt some traditional educational practices which shape the usual production of academic work. Quite deliberately, for example, I chose to write in the form of autobiography, using the letter format as a means of moving me closer to readers. My decision to write about abuse followed my earlier plan to write about battered women. Theoretically, I felt I could not analyze how women experience and reproduce abuse without first understanding how I experience and reproduce abuse.

The data base for my research is drawn from a variety of sources. Primarily, I draw from personal memories recreated in story form. I use these stories as a means of thinking about and analyzing my experiences of abuse. In a similar way, I use the three essays, completed prior to my decision to address my abuse, as important points of reference. These essays are interesting because they mark my struggle to emerge from years of silence. In a sense, these essays signal my preparedness to confront the abuses done to me.

Common to the titles and themes of the three papers are preoccupations with absenting, contradictions, harmony and margins. Retrospectively, because I had not learned to critique my own experiences of abuse I therefore produced and reproduced further abuse. I had not yet learned, for example, how to speak and write from a perspective which would enable me to respond in healthier ways to educators. In effect, my stories and essays signal a contradictory need to be both absent and present, especially in my writing.

Given that my history of abuse has taught me well how to acquiesce to authority figures, whether male or female, it was not surprising to discover that I re-experienced feelings of abuse within learning environments organized in hierarchical and authoritative ways, intentionally designed to teach objectivity based on a separation of intellect and emotion. As an abuse survivor, I had learned to separate my intellect and my emotions. It is understandable, therefore, that I reproduced my silence in a schooling environment: schooling practices reinforced what I had already learned through abuse.

I use my stories and essays to remember and critique various forms of abuse. I wrote to remember a self who was damaged, first through sexual abuse, and later through dispassionate and emotionless academic practices and discourses. From these remembering exercises my aim is to open up space to devise creative methods of teaching, methods which could empower all students, female and male, to know themselves as producers and reproducers of knowledge.

Should this read like a success story of how one woman became the teacher she always wanted to be, or how one woman is coming to know herself as a writer, I apologize. This is not my intent, though my accomplishments do give me pleasure and an improved sense of self-worth. Such an interpretation would not do justice to the work presented here. It would also obscure the fact that, like many women academics, my first year of teaching may be my last. Like many junior scholars I am, after one year of teaching, about to join the ranks of sessional appointees; different cities, different provinces, rewarded by little pay and abundant work. That is, of course, unless I choose to be re-trained for a kind of work other than teaching, which I do with passion and love.

Given the few academic positions available, and the rigid construction of such positions, I may, in fact choose another kind of work. Making the choice, however, does not guarantee me work. Our society ensures these kinds of contradictions. Yet, given the responsibilities of maintaining a lone-parent household, and my desire for comforts such as food, clothing, and a roof over our heads, I must consider my options. Of course, the limits on my choices make me angry. Having just completed twelve years of post-secondary studies, why not?

In asking these kinds of political questions I am alerted to yet another question. Why do I assume that I must change myself to fit a society which in its very organization is illusory? In other words, how was I taught to believe that desire and possibility are 'natural' correlates in a democratic society? Why did I not learn instead to critique the illusions of a democratic system organized by relations of power and capital? Why did I not learn *how* to change society to better meet the needs and desires of all and not just of a privileged few?

I am not arguing here for the *right* to do a certain kind of work or even for the right to imagine how society might be better organized. Rather, I am attempting to demonstrate the need for schooling practices which enable students to critique the constructedness of any illusion. Key to these practices is a critique of how specific social practices teach us simultaneously to construct and desire in *illusory* ways and to believe that our failure to live these illusions is located in individual rather than social failure.

In schooling environments designed to reproduce the status quo, it is an illusion that students will be taught 'naturally' to critique the constructedness of knowledge and the practices and ideologies producing and reproducing relations of power. In fact, teachers, like students, must be taught to critique the social organization of knowledge. This, of course, requires schooling practices which enable everyone to examine personal assumptions, emotions, ideas and privileges which shape practice and theory in a public way. Only through these kinds of practices will students like myself be taught to know abuse as a socially-organized practice rather than an individual failure. This analysis applies to both myself and my brother, who was also taught an illusion: that it was his right to abuse.

Schooling practices which empower students and teachers can be implemented in quite simple and obvious ways, once teachers agree to the importance of this work. What we need to do, I think, is to critique our positions of power and privilege as well as our positions of fear and inadequacy. This is difficult but not impossible work. To do this is to begin facing students as real people whose ideas are shaped and informed by particular social histories. The goal is to learn in ways which will clarify these histories. I am not advocating here that content is not important. Rather, I am calling for a kind of dialectical learning which will enable teachers and students to examine theories from the perspective of personal histories. Key to this way of learning is a recognition of how our perspectives are informed by need, desire, pain, emotion, trauma and joy.

I think this kind of learning depends upon our willingness and ability to teach students to read and write in ways which allow them to emotionally experience the theories and ideologies to which they are exposed. Presupposed, of course, is that most educators, like most students, will experience joy and motivation when taught to relate social theory and social practice in such ways as to critique and thus move beyond trauma and fear. This requires that we as students and teachers learn to name our fears and our joys in educational settings and in societies organized to produce silence and fear. Silent and fearful, we remain only dutiful subjects unable to care for ourselves or others.

Contradictorily, while I argue against social inequalities, I acknowledge the privileges which enable me to write about abuse. As a white, middle-class woman, I recognize in a painful way that I can write in this manner because of certain privileges, not least of which is access to education, safe places, the support of many women and a few men, the support of (mostly non-black) teachers, and an ongoing series of therapists. This support network presupposes privileged access to capital, class and power. In recognizing this privilege I am reminded constantly of, and angry about, the great injustices done to me; to people of colour; and to millions of women who suffer from abuse, whether it be sexual or that done through male-organized schooling practices. In the face of these abuses, I have chosen to sustain my anger until all women and men are abuse-free, else my words of recognition remain empty and I remain privileged despite my abuse.

Equally infuriating, I find, are depictions of women as silent and passive victims. Abused women like myself are damaged. Every day we live and confront this damage. But if through your reading of my words you imagine that I and other abuse survivors have lived our lives as silent victims, I will feel that I have failed in this exercise. For years, I have refused to see myself as silent or as a victim, while living the restrictions of my victimization. I now perceive this contradiction as an example of how I am coming to know myself as a meaning-maker in a world organized to make my work very difficult and sometimes impossible. I suspect this to be the case with many survivors of male abuse.

Similarly, and contradictorily, I live my power and my powerlessness. Through absenting I learned early to use the only power available to me. It is a power I now celebrate from a place of choice. Am I grateful for this? Yes, and no. I remember always the women I meet whose wills are broken, who are unable to resist. For such women we must all speak. Yet, there is an important aspect to even the silence of a broken will, a silence which, too, may be a choice. My not speaking of sexual abuse, for example, was at one level both a choice and an act of resistance. I chose not to tell my stories of abuse because I knew that potentially I might be unfairly judged or not believed. I chose to keep the integrity I knew. In this sense, I was neither a victim nor silenced. I chose to be silent. Yet the conditions of this choice are those of the oppressor. This I learned through writing my thesis.

Through writing, I began to see better the conditions of my oppression. As experienced in relationship to power, I am developing a clearer understanding of my abuse in an even more refined relationship of power: that of schooling practices which produce and reproduce hierarchy and authority. I write here about formal schooling practices which taught me further (than that already learned through abuse) to absent myself in my writing and reading practices, in the name of objectivity and reason. These kinds of practices taught me to censor identification with both myself and with the subject matter of my inquiries. Such practices led me to bifurcate a self already split. Writing has enabled me to see (once again) how these socially-constructed splits work upon me. And, in this re-view, I am able to see differently,

> that what I've experienced for so long as a personal split, and a severe sense of personal inadequacy, is anything but personal. It is produced by the very structure of academe in which we are bound (Rockhill, 1986:16).

I knew that I could not write about my experiences of abuse in an abstract and objective manner. I did not want to write without feeling about abuses which changed my life, which stole so much of my passion, desire, energy, and love of the everyday ordinary (Robinson, 1980). Yet, I sensed that if I did not write of my abuse, I would continue to reproduce my inability to care and feel, and trust what I know. I suspect that the educated makers of atom bombs, for example, learned to work in a similar way: work detached from its effects; work disconnected from social responsibility; work which we learn to do through non-critical educational practices.

Like many battered women, I was prepared to put up with my own abuse but not with the abuse of others. I do not speak here of altruism but rather of social constructedness. When faced with writing about battered women in a way I knew did not do justice to the everyday lives of these women, I resisted. I deeply resisted being told to write in an abstract and impersonal manner, though I was not at all sure why (then). I recall resisting as a deeply-felt bodily discomfort. I knew, moreover, that I did not want to write about battered women using the skills of abstraction and detachment which I had been taught. This I sensed would further de-personalize me and them.

It was this discomfort, I think, which inspired my desire to write differently. This meant that I needed to write first about my own history of abuse. Having now completed my autobiographical/theoretical/fictional account, I wonder how any researcher or educator can examine their own assumptions and biases, or those of others, without first examining, in writing, the assumptions and biases which organize their own teaching and learning practices.

In struggling to understand my difficulty with writing about battered women, I began to look for forms which would enable me to express with passion and care my own experiences of abuse. For this reason I chose to write letters as the basis of this autobiographical project. Letters, I know, are constructed to invite response. Essays are seldom written in this manner.

Love and Solidarity.

B: Another End(ing)

Since our aim is to reach a point at which we no longer see ourselves through the eyes of others, we have to take the risk of being seen to make mistakes. In our particular field, the weapon of defense we have chosen is writing (Haug et al., 1987:39).

Dear Lily, Andrew and Virginia:

Writing is, of course, a "weapon of defense" (Haug et al., 1987:39). In another sense, writing is a tool for creating new forms, images, words and ways. It was through the autobiographical work of Grumet that I first began to imagine the possibility of using my own words, in the form of autobiographical writing, to come to terms theoretically with the social practices of my past, and with the ghosts which taught me to absent myself in fear. Invisible, it was difficult to know or imagine myself as the creator of my own knowledge. Separated from this knowledge, I was also unable to know ideology as a social construct except in an (outer) intellectual way, a way which kept me from my inner visions. Using the memory-work and story-writing techniques of Haug et al. (1987), I began to envision ways of effecting social change through rewriting and recreating memories and experiences.

I have discussed how the writing and recognition of certain key words such as *absent* and *I was abused* enabled me to examine differently the abuses I had experienced first as a child and later in a schooling context. In particular, my aim was to analyze these abuses by writing stories which connect the events to a theoretical analysis of how I came to learn and develop in specific ways, ways which prevented me from viewing ideology as socially constructed. Having worked through these experiences, I am better able to see the implications of specific ideologies in my own social history and thus can choose if and how I want to engage in certain social practices. It was from this perspective, a place of choice, I suggest, that I began to reconsider ways of *doing* feminist pedagogy. In this sense, my work is about a "way of doing class" (Rockhill, 1985:2) which challenges conventional models of education.

C: Beginning Again: Doing Class

I wonder how we can talk about these issues that go so deep into the core of our being without looking critically at our experience. Can this be done in a **public forum**? As I get closer to the centre of women's oppression, which I believe is through our sexuality and its control through male-defined social forms and practices, I wonder how to open us up to critically examine our experiences without breaking trust, social taboos, or infringing upon our lives, uninvited (Rockhill, 1985:7).

So what does women's oppression and women's sexuality and sexual oppression through male-defined social forms and practices have to do with feminist pedagogy? Through a complex weaving of stories, narrations and analyses, I attempt to show how abuse affected me and how I see the effects of this abuse reproduced through masculine social forms and practices. For example, in learning to write in a detached and abstract manner, I was taught to comply with my oppressors, whose practices prevented me from writing or consciously knowing the abuses which shaped, organized and informed my developing subject self. Not able to write this abuse because of perceived social taboos, I was *silenced*, and I silenced myself.

Silenced, I implicitly agreed to the reproduction of the male-defined forms and practices which explicitly organized me (despite my on-going resistance to these forms). Silenced, I maintained the status quo. This method worked so very well because I accepted the illusions of the male-organized society which believes that I was to blame. Similarly, these illusions work to silence women who struggle to break free of the social relations and practices which produce and reproduce silence, abuse, and violence. I used the work of my thesis to break some of the silences organizing me. I could not have done this work without access to feminist perspectives and pedagogies.

But what, you ask again, does all this have to do with feminist pedagogy? How do I understand feminist pedagogy? The answers to these questions are complex. Weiler in her book *Women Teaching for Change* is, according to Giroux and Freire, attempting to develop "a critical theory of schooling that illuminates how gender is socially constructed with institutional and ideological technologies of power that inform all aspects of school life" (1988:iv). For me, the strength of Weiler's work lies in her analysis of how certain feminist instructors attempt to problematize gender, race and class within what she terms the feminist classroom. Working from her own interests, her study focuses on the practices of women instructors struggling in the classroom "against patriarchal hegemony and who seek to encourage among students a critical consciousness of sexism and roles of men and women" (148). While reading Weiler's excellent analysis of feminist teaching practices, I wanted to understand more fully how and why women choose to work from feminist perspectives.

The question of why I think feminist pedagogies are important is central to this book. In keeping with Williamson, I suggest that a critical feminist pedagogy requires that students understand, from a focus on their own experiences, how ideology is socially organized. This involves "not so much saying new things but saying the same basic things again and again" (1981/82:81). From my perspective, this means a continual taking up of power relations through writing, reading and discussion. Williamson argues that it is of little importance what we teach, as long as it leads to questioning of the assumptions which inform our social practices. I agree. Herein, she suggests, lies the potential for social change (83). It is this kind of questioning, she posits, which can also lead to discomfort, disquiet and crises in the classroom. To meet this sort of reaction to critical pedagogy, I think we must develop practical ways of contending with these eruptions; we must not avoid or soothe them away. It is, after all, these which, once dealt with, may inspire a student or teacher to begin learning in a meaningful way.

For this reason, I suggest that instructors who want to take up this kind of work (and if we don't, what are we teaching, really?) must be prepared to work with contradictions and crises. I argue that instructors interested in working from feminist perspectives must be taught how to examine and work with the ghosts of their past and present lives, else they will not be able to work with the ghosts of their students' lives in a safe and caring manner. While many of the ghosts of my own past are located in abuse, my stories are but one example of how social experiences can affect learning and development within academe. What is important, I suggest, is that we learn to work with our respective experiences in order to understand how they shape our teaching and learning abilities and practices.

I have discussed how various kinds of CR practices and autobiographical writing practices could be used to guide our reflections and analyses of past ghosts and thus improve our present learning. This is work which, in contrast with Belenky et al. (1986), can be taken up immediately, in any classroom, with both women and men, without devising a whole new curriculum (Brookes, 1988). The problems of integrating a feminist perspective located in women's everyday experience into existing educational practices are, as many educators know, monumental. These problems and resistances to integration are documented and discussed in the work of Aiken et al. (1987).

While I began in part, from the assumption that educators are working for change within existing educational practices, I know also the power of co-optation and the need to work from both the margin and the centre of practices which promote both liberation and oppression. The problem of how to work differently with practices organized to teach oppression cannot, of course, be solved at the level of the individual. This is collective work which must always be related to larger social change. If, however, we can use our schools to help students and instructors see how we are organized to oppress, through practices such as silencing, loving, forgiving, optimism, and fearing, we might begin to shift the foundations upon which our illusions are built. This is a difficult work, especially in a society which uncritically teaches both social inequality and democracy.

Crucial to the feminist perspectives with which I organize my own teaching practices is my attempt to take up relations of power, sexuality, gender, race, and class through concurrent readings of fiction and theory. Based on the experiences described in Chapter 7, I believe reader-response in any capacity is intricately and intimately tied to how we reproduce knowledge, precisely because its focus is reader agency. In other words, by teaching students to value their own reader agency — their experience of the text — we can begin to teach students how to construct and make meaning through the mediation of the texts, and from a perspective located in their own experiences. In this way, we are able to provide spaces in which students can view, from their own experiences, the social constructedness of ideology and knowledge.

Through the writing of letters, essays and critiques which address how fiction and theory are constructed, from the perspective of individual student experiences, I suggest we can teach students how to address issues of relevance to their own lives. Through discussions, writing, reading, and research, power can be understood and critiqued in the context of described social experience, including that which is personal to both students and teachers. That these experiences might include sexual abuse or any kind of trauma not previously discussed in public spaces potentially allows for the diffusion and dissolution of those social practices responsible for the existence and silencing of such abuse. It is this kind of experience, I suggest, which teaches students to work from, and develop further, feminist pedagogies and perspectives.

Lastly, I want to share with you a letter I wrote to a friend during the very early stages of writing the text you have just read:

Dear Lorna:

I am writing to you this morning because I am missing you but also because I want to tell you about my recent discovery of Madeleine Grumet's work. In particular, I am excited by her methodological use of *autobiography* and story as a device for understanding how it is that theory is made. Her use of autobiography is exciting, I think, because it provides students, provides me, with an understanding of how to theorize experience. More specifically, autobiography seems like a wonderful way to examine and theorize education experience.

The implications of her method are exciting. As you know, for a number of years I have struggled with the question of first, *how* to put myself as researcher into the text, and second, *why* I think it is theoretically significant to do so. Dissatisfied with the current trend which uses introductions as a way of adding author intent and experience to a text, I have struggled with what it means to theorize from my own experience: as a researcher, with all kinds of informing social experience, shaping the materials and matters which I critically assess and describe.

In particular, I am excited by Grumet's use of the autobiographical form because I imagine it will permit me as both student and instructor to better understand subjective formations and how theory is developed by subjects informed by subject matter. Without this information, I seem forever bound to the idea that knowledge is socially constructed, without knowing how and why. The strength of Grumet's work lies in her ability to put human experience and agency front and centre through concrete writing practices based on personal experiences, from which to then address theory in general. As a methodological exercise, Grumet's attention to autobiography is an exciting means of exploring and analyzing social experience.

In a concrete way, my excitement is informing my current work. Enclosed is a copy of my most recent thesis proposal, which I wrote last fall prior to reading Grumet's work. Despite my extensive knowledge of the battered women's shelter movement, I have been unable to write and organize this material into a form which reflects both the data available to me and the changes in my thinking since I first became interested in the movement. My frustration is located in my inability to present the stories of battered women as they were willingly and trustingly told to me. How can I ever write about the horrible experiences which many women have shared with me? Each time I listen to another woman's story, I find myself confronting a question which pervades the literature on battering: why do women stay in these situations? While the reasons are varied and complex, I believe that women stay and are silent about their abuse because of the sophisticated ways in which *they* are taught, through a variety of social practices to not speak about, to not know, the atrocities done to them. It is the relations of these illusions we must work to understand, I suggest. Having said this, I find myself producing yet another thesis proposal.

In my current work, I am struggling with the desire to write in a way which reflects both what I know and how I know; how my educational experiences, both within and apart from academe, shape the ways in which I know; how I and others produce knowledge. Yet each attempt to write a proposal which takes up the problem of critical consciousness in relation to battered women brings me back to data as the ultimate and informing authority. This is despite my attempts to create some kind of dialogue between the data and my organization of it. I have not been able to methodologically get my head around a way of making legitimate what I want: to develop a theoretical perspective from which to examine the relationship of subjectivity to the construction of theory. Rather than working primarily with consciousness raising as a basis for my research, I want to use autobiography as a way of organizing my writing. For a long while I hesitated to ask questions from my own experience. I kept looking for a legitimate way to study the battered women's movement, refusing to take seriously the question of why and how I am motivated and interested in a particular subject, let alone how it is that I know, and what I know.

For the past few weeks I have been ranting and raving about a recently published book (Belenky et al., 1986) in which, I think, the authors erroneously assume that women have a different way of knowing than men, a way related to our educational experiences, particularly those which shape women outside of academic settings, as in the case of sexual abuse. This book bothers me for a number of reasons. With the book, I am sending along a copy of my review of it. What I do not address in this review, however, is my frustration with a sort of mystification which, I think, informs this text and the authors' assumptions that all will be well when we construct a model of education based upon women's different maternal practices. Like so many educational studies, it is one which demands that we construct yet another new model of education.

By contrast, what I like about the work of Grumet is her attempt to develop a way of teaching students about social differences: by using students' own writings to critique assumptions and to examine, through autobiographical work, the relationship of practice to theory. From this kind of work, Grumet has devised ways of examining ideological formations, theoretical assumptions and theories of these formations from what I would call a *here and now* perspective. I find exciting her ability to begin from where we are as researchers, instructors, and students in the context of our current academic practices, rather than from an abstracted ideal which we can only strive to attain after the fact. More excitingly, her recent work indicates a concerted effort to come to terms with gender differences as related to the production of social theory. For certain this work will be helpful as we develop further our feminist perspectives. All of my interest in her work presumes, however, that such a method will be used to disrupt the existing and troublesome relations of power between students and instructors who are not taught and who choose not to take up issues of power, sexuality, gender, race, and class in the context of our everyday practices.

Love and Solidarity.

When I wrote this letter I was not (yet) prepared to write the book I have just completed. It was not until I read Rockhill (1985, 1986, 1987) and took seriously the ideas in her texts that I allowed myself to imagine writing from my own perspective, located and contextualized in my experience as an abuse survivor. Now that I have completed this work, I fear that in my attempts to theorize the relationship of sexual abuse to my learning and development, I have allowed an element of *essentialism* into my analysis. This is not intended. In attempting to link my experiences of abuse to a theoretical explanation of how educational practices, particularly with respect to relations of power and authority, can work to reproduce silence and maintenance of the status quo, my aim is to break a kind of sequencing and silencing which prevents victims of abuse from remembering and naming the social practices which oppress. While my focus is on the oppression of women through sexual abuse, I write also to confront the schooling practices which work to further split both women and men who have already learned mind and body splits in response to various kinds of trauma. In remembering my own splits, my intent is to create, and implement, pedagogical practices which enable students to identify the social constructedness of embodied ideological splits.

D: Endings of Another Kind

> I picked flowers and bright early fall leaves, for my lover, and thought about how I could not finish this article . . . convincingly, finally. So? **The End** (Corrigan, 1988:21).

> That night I dream I am dancing to Stevie Wonder's song "Always" (the name of the song is really "As," but I hear it as "Always"). As I dance, whirling and joyous, happier than I've ever been in my life, another bright-faced dancer joins me. We dance and kiss each other and hold each other through the night. The other dancer has obviously come through all right, as I have done. She is beautiful, whole and free. And she is also me (Walker, 1984:393).

I like these endings. They appeal to my newly (re)discovered sense of exploration, of how to think about new forms, openness and being closed, and learning, re-learning, remembering and re-membering.

Love and Solidarity.

references

Aiken, Susan Hardy, Anderson, Karen, Dinnerstein, Myra, Lensink, Judy, & MacCordquodale, Patricia. Trying transformations: Curriculum integration and the problem of resistance. *Signs, 12* (2), 255-275.

Ashton-Warner, Sylvia (1963). *Teacher.* New York: Simon and Schuster.

Atwood, Margaret (1983). *Bluebeard's egg.* Toronto: Seal Books.

Atwood, Margaret (1985). *The handmaid's tale.* Toronto: McLelland & Stewart.

Backhouse, Constance & Cohen, Leah (1978). *The secret oppression: sexual harassment of working women.* Toronto: MacMillan.

Barthes, Roland (1979). From work to text. In Josue V. Harari (Ed.), *Textual strategies: Perspectives in post-structuralist criticism* (73-81). Ithaca: Cornell University Press.

Batsleer, Janet, Davies, Tony, O'Rourke, Rebecca, & Weedon, Chris (1985). *ReWriting English: Cultural politics of gender and class.* London:Methuen.

Beaudry, Micheline (1985). *Battered women.* Montreal: Black Rose Books.

Belenky, Mary Field, Clinchy, Blythe McVicker, Goldberger, Nancy Rule, & Tarule, Jill Mattuck (1986). *Women's ways of knowing: The development of self, voice and mind.* New York: Basic Books.

Belsey, Catherine (1980). *Critical practice.* London: Methuen.

Belsey, Catherine (1982). Re-reading the great tradition. In Peter Widdowson (Ed.), *Re-reading English* (121-135). London: Methuen.

Breines, Wini and Gordon, Linda (1983). The new scholarship on family violence. *Signs, 8* (3), 490-531.

Brodkey, Linda (1987, January). Writing ethnographic narratives. *Writing Communication, 4* (1), 25-50.

Brookes, Anne-Louise (1982). *Ritual process in a women's transition house: Conjuring a new social paradigm.* Unpublished master's thesis, University of New Brunswick.

Brookes, Anne-Louise (1988). [Review of *Women's ways of knowing: The development of self, voice, and mind*]. *Curriculum Inquiry, 18* (1), 113-121.

Brookes, Anne-Louise, Ross, Becki (1986). *Letters from Becki and Anne-Louise.* Available from Anne-Louise Brookes, Department of Sociology, St. Francis Xavier University, Antigonish, Nova Scotia).

Cambridge Women's Peace Collective. (1984). *My country is the whole world: An anthology of women's work on peace and war.* London: Pandora Books.

Campbell, Patsy (1987). *Personal Correspondence.* (Available from Anne-Louise Brookes, Department of Sociology, St. Francis Xavier University, Antigonish, Nova Scotia).

Chodorow, Nancy (1978). *The reproduction of mothering: Psychoanalysis and the sociology of gender.* Berkeley: University of California Press.

Christ, Carol P. (1980). *Diving deep and surfacing: Women writers on spiritual quest.* Boston: Beacon Press.

Corrigan, Philip (1984, Fall). Doing mythologies. *border/lines*, 20-22.

Corrigan, Philip (1987). In forming Schooling. In David Livingstone (Ed.), *Critical Pedagogy and cultural power.* South Hadley: Bergin & Garvey Publishers.

Corrigan, Philip (1987). *Masculinity as right: some thoughts on the genealogy of 'rational violence'.* Unpublished manuscript, Ontario Institute for Studies in Education, Department of Sociology of Education, Toronto.

Corrigan, Philip (1987). The body of intellectuals/the intellectual's body (remarks for Roland). *Sociological Review.*

Corrigan, Philip (1987, March). *Education for masculinity.* Paper presented in Santiago, Chile.

Corrigan, Philip (1988). "Innocent stupidities...": De-picturing (human) nature.

On hopeful resistances, and possible refusals: celebrating difference(s)___again. In G. Frye & J. Law (Eds.), *On visuality*. London: Routledge and Kegan Paul.

Culleton, Beatrice (1983). *In search of April Raintree*. Winnipeg: Pemmican Publications.

Delaney, Sheila (1983). *Writing women: Women writers and women in literature, medieval to modern*. New York: Schocken Books.

DeSalvo, Louise (1989). Virginia Woolf: The Impact of Childhood Sexual Abuse on her Life and Work. Boston: Beacon Press.

Dobash, R. & Dobash, Russell P. (1979). *Violence against wives: A case against the patriarchy*. New York: Free Press.

Dreyfus, Hubert L. & Rabinow, Paul (1982). *Michel Foucault: beyond structuralism and hermeneutics*. Chicago: University of Chicago Press.

Duplessis, Rachel Blau (1985). *Writing beyond the ending: narrative strategies of twentieth-century women writers*. Bloomington: Indiana University Press.

Eichler, Margit (1983). *The relationship between sexist, non-sexist, feminist and woman-centred research*. Paper presented at the meeting of the American Sociological Association.

Franklin, Ursula Martius (1984). Will women change technology or will technology change women? In June I. Gow and Willadean Leo (Eds.), *Knowledge reconsidered: A feminist overview*. Ottawa: CRIAW.

Fraser, Sylvia (1987). *My father's house: A memoir of incest and of healing*. Toronto: Doubleday.

Freire, Paulo (1970). *Pedagogy of the oppressed (Myra Bergman Ramos, Trans.)* New York: Herder and Herder. (Original work published 1968).

Freire, Paulo (1973). *Education for critical consciousness*. New York: Herder and Herder.

French, Marilyn (1977). *The women's room*. New York: Jove/HBJ Books.

Gilbert, Sandra M. (1983). Soldier's heart: Literary men, literary women and the great war. *Signs, 8* (3), 422-450.

Gilligan, Carol (1982). *In a different voice: Psychological theory and women's development*. Cambridge: Harvard University Press.

Gilman, Charlotte Perkins (1973). *The yellow wallpaper.* Afterword by Elaine R. Hedges. New York: The Feminist Press.

Grumet, Madeleine (1979). Supervision and situation. *Journal of Curriculum Theorizing, 1.*

Grumet, Madeleine (1981). Autobiography and reconceptualization. In Henry Giroux, Anthony N. Penna & William Pinar (Eds.) *Curriculum and instruction.* Berkeley: McCutchan.

Grumet, Madeleine (1981). Conception, contradiction and curriculum. *Journal of Curriculum Theorizing, 3* (1), 287-298.

Grumet, Madeleine (1981). Restitution and reconstruction of educational experience: An autobiographical method for curriculum theory. In M. Lawn & L. Barton (Eds.), *Rethinking curriculum studies: A radical approach.* New York: John Wiley.

Grumet, Madeleine (1985). *Teaching the text: Trapped in transference or gypped again.* Unpublished manuscript, University of Rochester, Graduate School of Education and Human Development, Rochester.

Grumet, Madeleine (1986). The Paideia proposal: A thankless child. *Curriculum Inquiry, 16* (3), 335-344.

Guberman, Connie & Wolfe, Margie (Eds.) (1985). *No safe place.* Toronto: Women's Press.

Hanscombe, Gillian E. (1982). *Between friends.* Boston: Alyson Publications.

Haug, Frigga (Ed.) (1987). *Female sexualization* (Erica Carter, Trans.). London: Verso. (Original work published 1983).

Kelly, Ursula (1986, November). *Reading for social change: Toward an emancipatory pedagogy.* Paper presented at the annual conference of the National Council of Teachers of English, San Antonio.

Kelly, Ursula (1986). *Reading from the margins: A feminist analysis of the fallout.* Unpublished manuscript, Ontario Institute for Studies in Education, Department of Curriculum, Toronto.

Kincaid, Pat J. (1982). *The omitted reality.* Maple, ON: Publishing and Printing Services.

Kolodny, Annette (1985). A map for re-reading: Gender and the interpretation of literary texts. In Elaine Showalter (Ed.). *The new feminist criticism: Essays on women, literature and theory* (46-62). New York: Pantheon Books.

Lane, Ann J. (1980). *The Charlotte Perkins Gilman reader.* New York: Pantheon Books.

Lewis, Magda & Roger I. Simon. A Discourse Not Intended for Her: Learning and Teaching Within Patriarchy. *Harvard Educational Review, 56* (4).

Lewis, Magda (1988). *Without a word: Sources and themes for a feminist pedagogy.* Unpublished doctoral dissertation, The Ontario Institute for Studies in Education, University of Toronto.

Livingstone, David W. (Ed.) (1987). *Critical pedagogy and cultural power.* South Hadley: Bergin & Garvey Publishers.

MacLeod, Linda (1980). *Wife battering in Canada: The vicious circle.* Ottawa: Supply and Services Canada.

McIntyre, Sheila (1986). *Memo.* (Available from Sheila McIntyre, Faculty of Law, Queen's University, Kingston, ON.)

McIntyre, Sheila (1987, January). Gender bias within a Canadian law school. *CAUT Bulletin ACPU,* 7-11.

McMahon, Marion (1986). *Things that haunt me when I write.* Unpublished manuscript, Ontario Institute for Studies in Education, Department of Sociology of Education, Toronto.

Mead, Margaret (1949). *Male and female: A study of the sexes in a changing world.* New York: William Morrow.

Meese, Elizabeth A. (1986). *Crossing the double-cross: The practice of feminist criticism.* Chapel Hill: University of North Carolina Press.

Meigs, Mary (1981). *Lily Briscoe: A self-portrait: An autobiography.* Vancouver: Talon Books.

Mitchell, Juliet & Oakley, Ann (Eds.) (1986). *What is feminism?* Oxford: Basil Blackwell.

O'Brien, Mary (1981). *The politics of reproduction.* Boston: Routledge & Kegan Paul.

Oakley, Ann. (1986). *Telling the truth about Jerusalem.* London: Basil Blackwell.

Okum, Lewis (1986). *Woman abuse: Facts replacing myths.* Albany: State University of New York.

Ortega Y Gasset, Jose (1932). *The revolt of the masses.* New York: W.W. Norton & Co.

Paget, Marianne A. (1987). *For feminist discourse.* (Available from Marianne A. Paget, Law and Social Science Program, Northwestern University, 2040 Sheridan Road, Evanston, Illinois, 60208).

Perry, William (1970). *Forms of intellectual and ethical development in the college years.* New York: Holt, Rinehart & Winston.

Pinar, W. & Grumet, M. (1976). *Toward a poor curriculum.* Dubuque: Kendall Hunt.

Pizzey, Erin (1974). *Scream quietly or the neighbours will hear.* Middlesex: Penguin Books.

Radway, Janice (1984). *Reading the romance: Women, patriarchy and popular literature.* Chapel Hill: University of North Carolina Press.

Rayman, Paula (1982). Utopian visions: Reflections on feminist and nonviolent thought. In Pam McAllister (Ed.), *Reweaving the web of life: Feminism and nonviolence.* Philadelphia: New Society Press.

Roberts, Barbara (1983). No safe place: The war against women. *Our Generation, 15* (4), 7-26.

Robinson, Marilynne (1981). *Housekeeping.* New York: Bantam Books.

Rockhill, Kathleen (1985, November). *Memorandum to participants of 1112.* (Available from Kathleen Rockhill, Department of Adult Education, The Ontario Institute for Studies in Education, Toronto).

Rockhill, Kathleen (1986, April). *The chaos of subjectivity.* Paper presented at the Feminist Lecture Series, Toronto.

Rockhill, Kathleen (1987). Literacy as threat/desire: Longing to be SOMEBODY. In Jane S. Gaskell & Arlene Tigar McLaren (Eds.), *Women and education: A Canadian perspective* (315-331). Calgary: Detselig Enterprises.

Rockhill, Kathleen (1987, March). *Violence against wives.* Paper presented at the School of Social Work, Toronto: University of Toronto.

Russ, Joanna (1983). *How to suppress women's writing.* London: The Women's Press.

Shaffer, Beverly, Rogers, Gerry, Shannon, Janes, Barbara, Strikeman, Ginny,

& Fraticelli, Rina (Producers), & Shaffer, Beverly (Director). (1987). *To a Safer Place* [Film]. National Film Board, Studio D.

Smith, Dorothy E. (1974). The Ideological practice of sociology. *Catalyst 8*, 39-54.

Smith, Dorothy E. (1974). Women's perspective as a radical critique of sociology. *Sociological Inquiry, 44* (1), 7-13.

Smith, Dorothy E. (1975). The Social construction of documentary reality. *Sociological Inquiry, 44* (4), 257-268.

Smith, Dorothy E. (1977). The intersubjective structure of time: An analysis of how it was done on a particular occasion. *Analytic Sociology, 1* (2).

Smith, Dorothy E.(1979). A sociology for women. In Julia A. Sherman & Evelyn Toronton Beck (Eds.), *The prism of sex: Essays in the sociology of knowledge*. Madison: University of Wisconsin Press.

Smith, Dorothy E. (1982). *The active text: A textual analysis of the social relations of public textual discourse*. Paper presented at the World Congress of Sociology, Mexico City.

Smith, Dorothy E. (1983). No one commits suicide: Textual analysis of ideological practices. *Human Studies, 6* 309-359.

Smith, Dorothy E. (1984). Textually mediated social organization. *International Social Science Journal, 36* (1), 59-75.

Smith, Dorothy E. (1987). *The everyday world as problematic: A feminist sociology*. Toronto: University of Toronto Press.

Spring, Jacqueline (1987). *Cry hard and swim*. London: Virago Press.

Stanley, Liz & Wise, Sue (1983). *Breaking out: Feminist consciousness and feminist research*. London: Routledge and Kegan Paul.

Steinson, Barbara J. (1980). The mother half of humanity: American women in the peace and preparedness movements in World War I. In Carol R. Berkin & Clara M. Lovett (Eds.), *Women, war & revolution* (259-284). New York: Holmes and Meier.

Swerdlow, Amy (1982). Ladies' day at the capitol: Women strike for peace versus HUAC. *Feminist Studies, 8* (3), 493-520.

Sydie, R.A. (1987). *Natural women, cultured men: A feminist perspective on sociological theory*. Toronto: Methuen.

Vallee, Brian (1986). *Life with Billy*. Toronto: Seal Books.

Volosinov, V.N. (1973). *Marxism and the philosophy of language* (Ladislav Matejka & I.R. Titunik, Trans.). New York: Seminar Press. (Original work published 1929)

Vygotsky, L.S. (1962). *Thought and language* (Eugenia Hanfmann & Gertrude Vakar, Trans.). Cambridge: MIT Press.

Walker, Alice (1967). *In search of our mothers' gardens*. San Diego: Harcourt Brace Jovanovich.

Warnock, Donna (1982). Patriarchy is a killer: What people concerned about peace and justice should know. In Pam McAllister (Ed.), *Reweaving the web of life: Feminism and nonviolence* (20-26). Philadelphia: New Society Publishers.

Weedon, Chris. (1987). *Feminist practice & poststructuralist theory*. London: Basil Blackwell.

Weiler, Kathleen (1988). *Women teaching for change: Gender, class & power*. South Hadley: Bergin & Garvey Publishers.

Williamson, Judith (1980). *Consuming passions: The dynamics of popular culture*. London: Marion Boyars.

Williamson, Judith (1981/82). How does girl number twenty understand ideology? *Screen Education, 40*, 80-87.

Wilson, Elizabeth (1983). *What is to be done about violence against women?* Middlesex: Penguin Books.

Woolf, Virginia (1938). *Three guineas*. London: Hogarth Press.